Greatest Athletes *of the* 20*th* Century

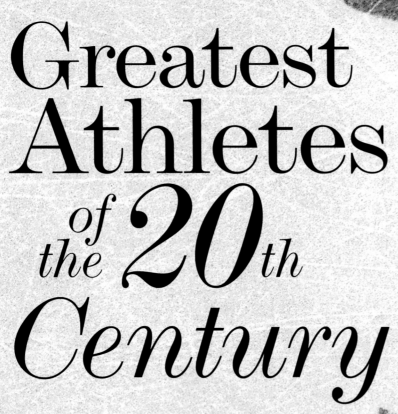

Greatest Athletes of the 20th Century

By Tim Crothers
and John Garrity

Total/SPORTS ILLUSTRATED and SPORTS ILLUSTRATED
are trademarks of Time Inc. Used under license.

For information about permission to reproduce selections from this book,
please write to:
Permissions
Total/SPORTS ILLUSTRATED
105 Abeel Street
Kingston, New York 12401

ISBN 1-892129-18-3
Library of Congress Catalog Card Number: 99-71060

GREATEST ATHLETES was prepared by
Bishop Books, Inc.
611 Broadway
New York, New York 10012

Printed in the United States of America

10 9 8 7 6 5 4 3 2 1

Contents

Introduction . . . . *.6*

Transcendent Three 8
Muhammad Ali . . . . *.12*
Michael Jordan . . . . *.20*
Babe Ruth . . . . *.28*

Peerless Performers 34
Wilt Chamberlain . . . . *.38*
Babe Didrikson . . . . *.44*
Wayne Gretzky . . . . *.50*
Rod Laver . . . . *.56*
Carl Lewis . . . . *.62*
Jack Nicklaus . . . . *.68*
Pelé . . . . *.74*
Bill Russell . . . . *.80*
Jim Thorpe . . . . *.86*
Ted Williams . . . . *.92*

Greatness Visible 98
Hank Aaron . . . . *.102*
Larry Bird . . . . *.108*
Jim Brown . . . . *.114*
Red Grange . . . . *.120*
Don Hutson . . . . *.126*
Magic Johnson . . . . *.132*
Jackie Joyner-Kersee . . . . *.138*
Joe Louis . . . . *.144*
Mickey Mantle . . . . *.150*
Willie Mays . . . . *.156*
Joe Montana . . . . *.162*
Martina Navratilova . . . . *.168*

Photo credits . . . . *.174*
Index . . . . *.174*

Introduction

Yes, we're smug, self-righteous, wrongheaded dolts. We've made a list of the 20th century's top athletes, and we've somehow left out Mark Spitz, the swimmer who won seven gold medals at the 1972 Olympics. We've got five basketball players on our list—20% of the total—but we couldn't find room for Oscar Robertson, the man who brought all-around perfection to the game. We've got the Olympic heptathlon queen Jackie Joyner-Kersee, but we don't have the great decathlon gold medalist, Rafer Johnson, or England's two-time Olympic decathlon champ, Daley Thompson. We have no cricket players or rugby stars (we're too parochial), few athletes from the first quarter of the century (we're too young), and no jockeys, sailors or race car drivers (we're not sure they're athletes).

Having admitted to these deficiencies, we humbly submit that our list of 25 is pretty solid. All the athletes in our Top 25, for example, would probably appear on anybody's Top 50 list. We haven't slipped in a recent hot shot like Karl Malone simply to sell books in Salt Lake City. And we haven't biased the list by including Bobby Jones, Byron Nelson and Ben Hogan, just because we happen to be knowledgeable about golf.

If we have failed, it is because 25 is an odd number in more than the literal sense. A Top 10 list would be easy—you'd go with nothing but icons of sport like Babe Ruth, Pelé, Michael Jordan and Muhammad Ali. One hundred would be even easier—you'd have room for a gymnast (Nadia Comaneci), a miler (Roger Bannister) and a skater or two (Sonja Henie and Dick Button).

But 25? Twenty-five is King Solomon ordering a child cut in half to satisfy competing claims of motherhood. Twenty-five is a hot dog and a beer for five bucks, and you've only got four. But we relished the challenge, and we think this group of 25 occupied rare air indeed.

A few words about methodology. No computers were used to compile our Top 25. Computers can store numbers, but no computer ever went home from the Boston Garden raving about the behind-the-backboard, left-handed finger-roll that Larry Bird slipped past the nostrils of Darryl Dawkins to send the game into overtime. Furthermore, statistical comparisons between generations can lead to false conclusions, i.e., that Mark McGwire is better than Babe Ruth. Instead, we went with our hearts and minds, making up lists based upon subjective criteria. The co-authors made their lists independently, as did the book's editors and researchers.

As luck would have it, 10 names appeared on all five lists. *Voila*, we had a base from which to proceed. In Step Two, we crossed out those athletes who appeared on only one or two lists—goodbye Gordie Howe, Ty Cobb, Nancy Lopez, Dan Marino, Kareem Abdul-Jabbar and Al Oerter, among others.

Then it got tricky, because the list-makers weren't all that happy with Step Two. One writer pleaded for Billie Jean King, pointing out that she influenced not just tennis but also society. ("She persuaded men that women were real athletes.") The other fought for the inclusion of Jerry Rice ("The greatest receiver in NFL history.")

We had to make some tough calls to whittle our list down to 25, but the selections of Bird (above) and Laver (opposite) were no-brainers.

Consideration was also given to Bob Beamon, whose mind-blowing long jump at the Mexico City Olympics lasted less than 10 seconds, run-up included.

The inexact science that was our procedure hit home when we finally reduced the list to 25, only to realize a few days later that we had forgotten Joe Louis. (Joe Louis!) Everyone agreed that Louis had to be on the list; so we somewhat arbitrarily jettisoned Oscar Robertson—not because he was the least of our Great 25, but

because we had too many basketball players. How could we keep Robertson while excluding Abdul-Jabbar, who was the most dominating college player ever and the alltime NBA scoring leader?

Sorry, Oscar.

With Robertson and his 31 points, 12 rebounds and 11 assists per game in 1961–62 (yes, he averaged a triple-double that season) gone, we put our Great 25 on paper. Instead of ranking them numerically, we decided to divide them into three categories. The first grouping we dubbed the Transcendent Three, and it's difficult to argue with our selections of Ruth, Jordan and Ali. Their combination of athletic superiority and cultural impact is, with the possible exception of Pelé, unmatched.

For the next tier, we considered athletes who had accomplished something that no one would ever duplicate. Hence, Wilt Chamberlain goes into our Peerless Performers category. Think anyone will ever score 100 points in an NBA game again? How about tennis's Grand Slam—will any male player turn that trick again? Possibly, but who will do it twice, as Rod Laver did in the 1960s? That player is not on the men's tour now, and don't hold your breath waiting for him. And the day someone scores 92 goals in an NHL season, or passes off for 163 assists, as Wayne Gretzky did, call Gary Bettman's great-great-grandchildren and tell them their ancestor's rule changes have finally borne fruit.

Our third category, Greatness Visible, encompasses the rest of the cream of the 20th century's crop. Someone may break Henry Aaron's record of 755 career home runs, but no one will surpass his dignity or his astounding consistency. It's hard to imagine, but one day there may be a greater Celtic than Bird, but that won't make the folks in Boston, or anywhere else, forget Larry Legend.

Whatever its flaws, we think our list stacks up just fine, thank you, against anyone else's. Quibble all you want about the categories. Moan about the exclusion of this hockey player or that horseshoe thrower. But please, share our pleasure in reviewing the achievements of the best 25 athletes of the expiring century.   —*J.G.*

Transcendent Three

Transcendent Three

We begin with the transcendent three—Ruth, Jordan and Ali. Their names are a kind of currency; their faces are as familiar as those of Einstein and Lenin, Lincoln and Mickey Mouse. A child of ten in Belgrade, looking at a silhouette of a man dunking a basketball, squeals, "Michael!" A grandfather in Nigeria sees the cocky mug of Ali on a postage stamp and smiles.

The test for transcendence is name recognition. The pollster will tell you that more Americans know that Babe Ruth played for the Yankees than can identify the current occupant of the White House. Ali, in the 1960s, was said to be the most widely-known person on the planet, well ahead of John F. Kennedy, Pope Paul VI, Brigitte Bardot, Chairman Mao or even Elvis.

To be transcendent, the athlete must also be universally recognizable. Joe Montana, great as he is, can walk the streets anywhere outside North America without turning a head. Laplanders can't pick Rod Laver out of a lineup of reindeer. Even Wayne Gretzky, who dominated his sport as much as any of our Big Three did theirs, doesn't fulfill this particular requirement for icon-hood.

The first athlete to seize this high ground was Ruth, whose gargantuan appetites and unprecedented baseball skills enthralled a burgeoning sports audience. Ruth was the first baseball player to earn more than the President of the United States. He was the first athlete to have a stadium built for him. He was the first to endorse cigarettes he didn't smoke, cereals he didn't eat and underwear he didn't wear. He was also probably the first athlete to sign a million autographs, or eat 18 hot dogs in a sitting. When Ruth hit his 500th career home run, in 1929, the *New York World* called it an accomplishment "to be bracketed with our skyscrapers, our university, our millions of automobiles as symbols of American greatness."

Ali was a symbol, too, but not only of American greatness. Ali's global appeal derived, in part, from his dissenter's view of American politics and from his conversion to Islam. Jordan, in contrast, achieved icon status by signing endorsement contracts and linking up with image-makers like director Spike Lee and shoemaker Phil Knight. Jordan's famous brow, beaded with sweat, is familiar to television viewers in Stockholm, Cairo and Brisbane. And his skywalking figure, fifteen stories tall in his Bulls jersey, graces the walls of buildings from Rio to Singapore.

When spacemen with telescopes know your uniform number—that's transcendence.   —J.G.

With a mixture of athletic brilliance and cultural impact, our first three athletes, Jordan (opposite), Ruth (above) and Ali, transcended the playing fields and arenas of their sports to become timeless icons.

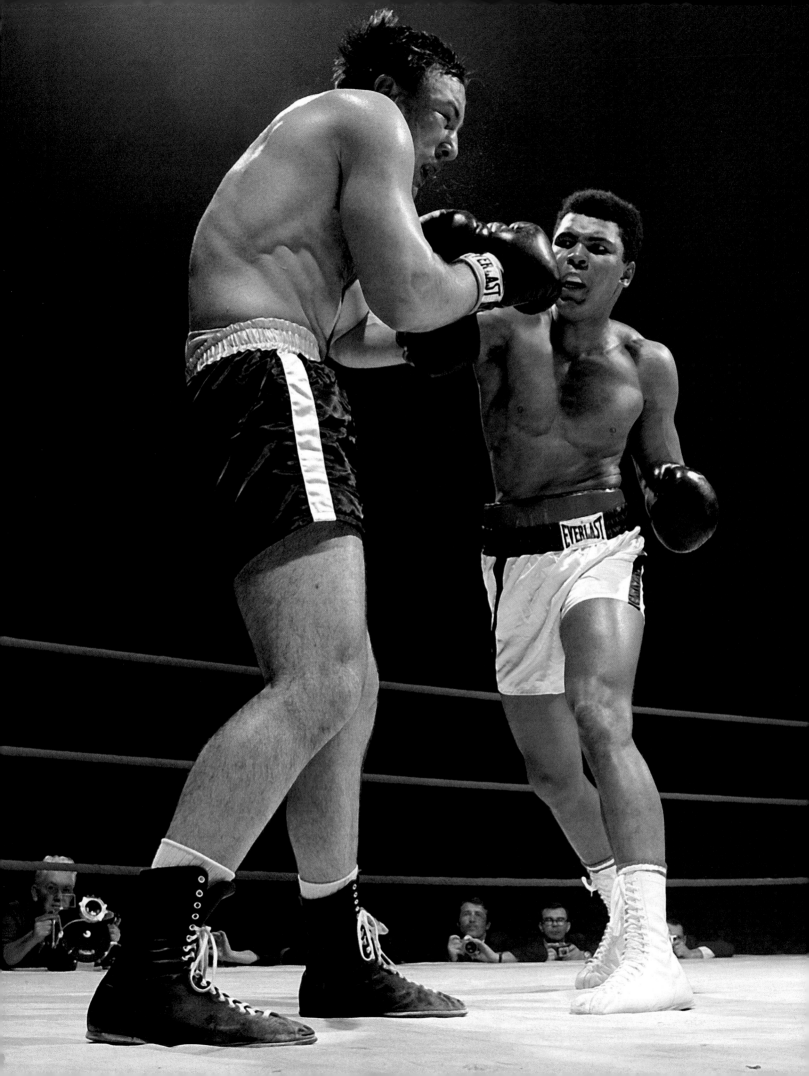

Muhammad Ali

One day Muhammad Ali informed the world that he was "the Greatest" because it was taking everybody too damn long to figure it out for themselves. He once described his fighting style in lyric verse: "Float like a butterfly, sting like a bee." He handicapped his third bout with Joe Frazier in dreadful verse: "It will be a killa and a chilla and a thrilla when I get the gorilla in Manila." The writers who were shadowing him tried to get a word in edgewise, tried to peek behind all the bluster at the man, but with Ali it was simpler to just sit back and let him do all the talking.

Whenever Ali spoke, planet Earth pricked up its ears. It wasn't always so much what he said as how he said it. He was part pugilist, part preacher and part poseur, and he reveled in everybody's struggle to divine what the heck he was really thinking behind all that blather and showmanship.

His name and much of his arrogance were acquired from his father Cassius Marcellus Clay, Sr., an amateur artist who painted murals in churches but earned his living painting signs. The younger Clay grew up in an old house on Grand Avenue in Louisville, where he regularly held court on his porch, regaling his neighbors with his lunatic fantasies. "You see this house?" he liked to say. "It's gonna be a shrine one day."

Sure enough, Clay won the light heavyweight boxing gold medal at the 1960 Olympics in Rome. In 1964, at the tender age of 22, he stunned the fearsome Sonny Liston to win the world heavyweight championship. He told anybody who would listen that he was the prettiest boxer around, and he started a tradition of asking for a mirror after his fights so that he could admire his unblemished features. He had learned this schtick from studying TV wrestler Gorgeous George. Clay began to not only predict victories but also had the temerity to predict the precise round of his opponent's demise. Fans originally showed up at his fights hoping to see the big mouth beaten, but their distaste eventually turned to respect and finally to admiration.

In Clay's prime, the only man that could take his title away worked for the Louisville Selective Service Board, a body that didn't take kindly to Clay's changing his name to

In his third successful heavyweight title defense, Ali (opposite, right) won a unanimous decision over George Chuvalo in Toronto in 1966.

Ali when he became a Muslim and then refusing to serve in Vietnam based on his religious convictions. While few Americans at the time supported a fighter who refused to fight in the war, Ali simply said, "I ain't got no quarrel with them Viet Cong." As punishment for refusing induction, Ali was stripped of his heavyweight title. Even though it wouldn't be long before the majority of Americans shared his views about the war, he was doomed to a 43-month exile from the ring.

Ali would come to transcend sports and become an almost political figure who was, and remains, instantly recognizable throughout the world. He had been alternately reviled and embraced by his own country, and therefore never hesitated to take his show on the road, doling out whuppings at points all around the globe. He was the athletic symbol of the tumultuous '60s and '70s, a proud man who had stared down the system and prevailed.

But Ali possessed far more than just a rapier tongue; he also owned the fastest hands and quickest feet ever bestowed upon a heavyweight. He was so agile for his size (6' 3") that he eschewed the customary fundamentals drilled into most fighters. He simply bobbed and weaved away from most punches. It also helped that his courage and ability to take a punch were unparalleled. While he was clearly not the most powerful heavyweight, he was a virtuoso boxer who showed a consistent and incredible ability to adjust his style to fit the opponent.

He won that first title against Liston in '64 with raw speed, youthful hubris and the Ali Shuffle. When he faced mighty George Foreman a decade later in Zaire, a fight dubbed the "Rumble in the Jungle," Ali took apart the bigger, stronger and younger Foreman with

m his triumph at the Olympics in Rome, the brash young Clay (above) trained at the 37th Street Gym in Miami in pursuit of the heavy-
ght title, which, at the peak of his powers in 1966, he ably defended with a third-round TKO of Cleveland Williams (opposite) in Houston.

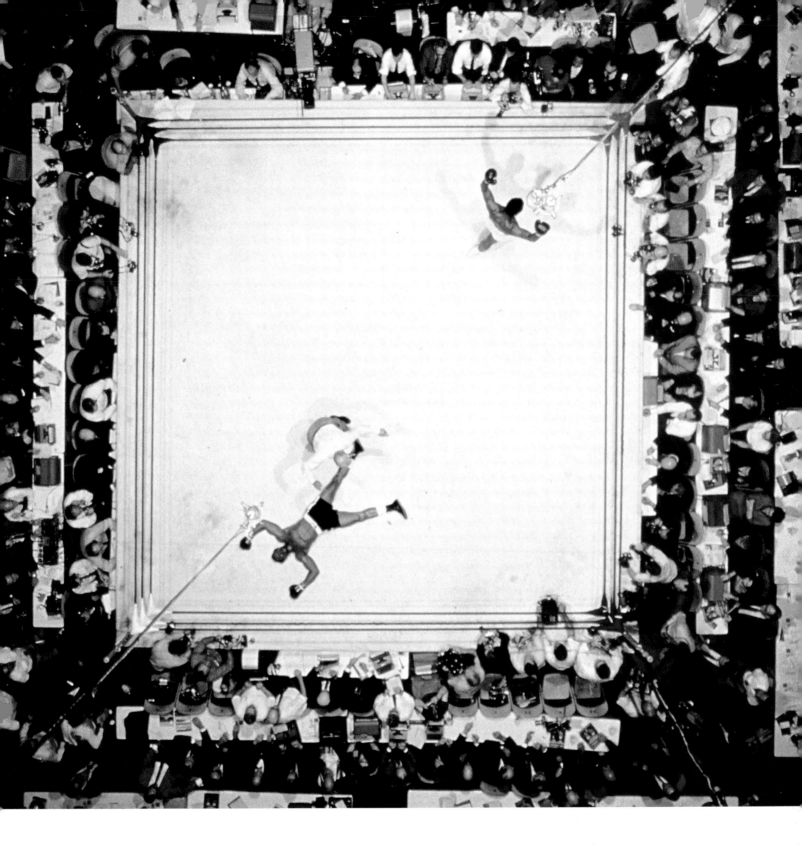

"We should have known that Muhammad Ali would not settle for any ordinary old resurrection. His had to have additional flourish. So, having rolled away the rock, he hit George Foreman on the head with it."

—*HUGH McILVANNEY, sportswriter, after the 1974 Ali-Foreman bout in Kinshasa, Zaire*

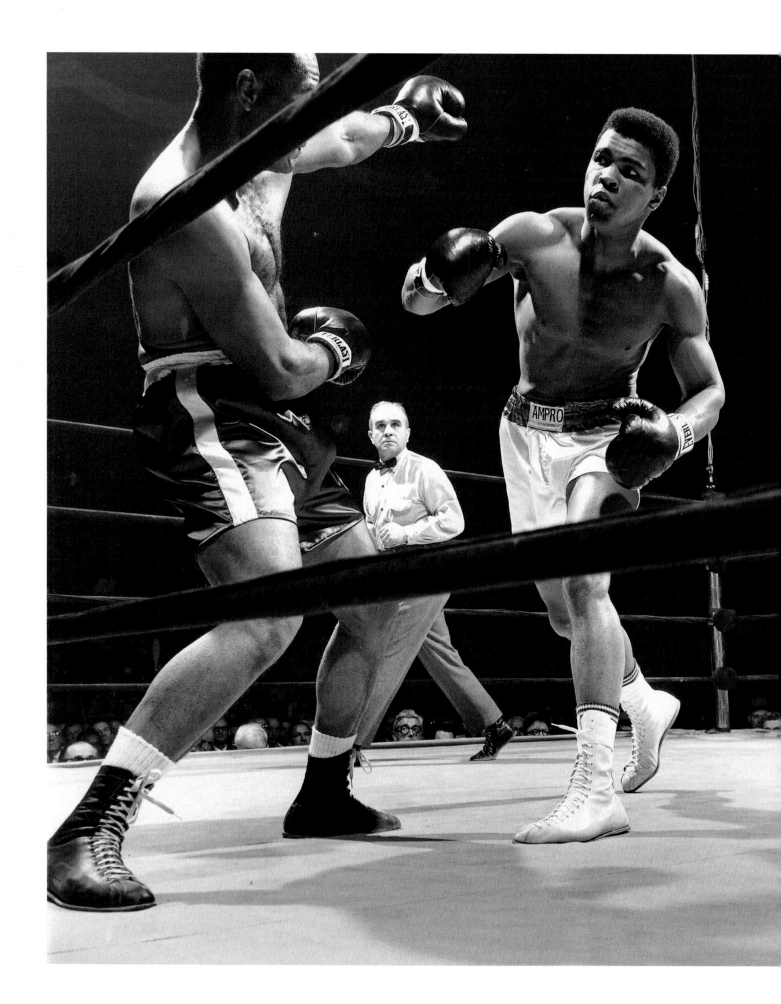

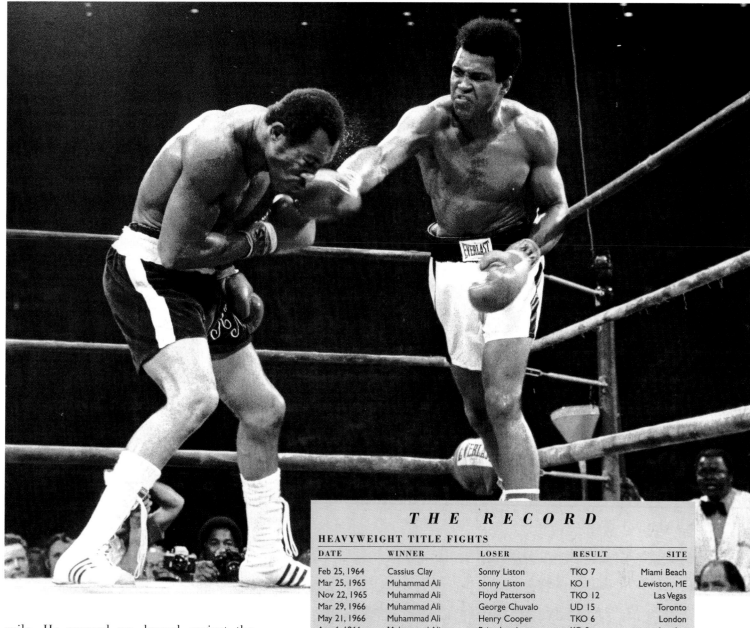

THE RECORD

HEAVYWEIGHT TITLE FIGHTS

DATE	WINNER	LOSER	RESULT	SITE
Feb 25, 1964	Cassius Clay	Sonny Liston	TKO 7	Miami Beach
Mar 25, 1965	Muhammad Ali	Sonny Liston	KO 1	Lewiston, ME
Nov 22, 1965	Muhammad Ali	Floyd Patterson	TKO 12	Las Vegas
Mar 29, 1966	Muhammad Ali	George Chuvalo	UD 15	Toronto
May 21, 1966	Muhammad Ali	Henry Cooper	TKO 6	London
Aug 6, 1966	Muhammad Ali	Brian London	KO 3	London
Sept 10, 1966	Muhammad Ali	Karl Mildenberger	TKO 12	Frankfurt
Nov 14, 1966	Muhammad Ali	Cleveland Williams	TKO 3	Houston
Feb 6, 1967	Muhammad Ali	Ernie Terrell WBA	UD 15	Houston
Mar 22, 1967	Muhammad Ali	Zora Folley	KO 7	New York City
Oct 30, 1974	Muhammad Ali	George Foreman	KO 8	Kinshasa, Zaire
Mar 24, 1975	Muhammad Ali	Chuck Wepner	TKO 15	Cleveland
May 16, 1975	Muhammad Ali	Ron Lyle	TKO 11	Las Vegas
July 1, 1975	Muhammad Ali	Joe Bugner	UD 15	Kuala Lumpur, Mal.
Oct 1, 1975	Muhammad Ali	Joe Frasier	TKO 15	Manila
Feb 20, 1976	Muhammad Ali	Jean Pierre Coopman	KO 5	San Juan
Apr 30, 1976	Muhammad Ali	Jimmy Young	UD 15	Landover, MD
May 24, 1976	Muhammad Ali	Richard Dunn	TKO 5	Munich
Sep 28, 1976	Muhammad Ali	Ken Norton	UD 15	New York City
May 16, 1977	Muhammad Ali	Alfredo Evangelista	UD 15	Landover, MD
Sept 29, 1977	Muhammad Ali	Earnie Shavers	UD 15	New York City
Feb 15, 1978	Leon Spinks	Muhammad Ali	Split 15	Las Vegas
Sept 15, 1978	Muhammad Ali	Leon Spinks	UD 15	New Orleans
Oct 2, 1980	Larry Holmes (WBC)	Muhammad Ali	TKO 11	Las Vegas

guile. He covered up, leaned against the ropes and let Foreman flail wildly. After seven rounds of this, Foreman had exhausted himself. Ali took him out in Round 8. The following year in Manila, Ali silenced his few remaining critics by proving he could win a toe-to-toe brawl on sheer guts, when he outlasted Frazier in the final fight of their remarkable trilogy.

As per boxing tradition, Ali retired several times, but the sport repeatedly demanded his return, and he simply could not resist the

Ali decked Zora Folley (opposite, left) in the seventh round of their 1967 title fight in New York City; six years later, in a return bout with Ken Norton (above, left), Ali took the decision to avenge an earlier loss to Norton in which he suffered a broken jaw.

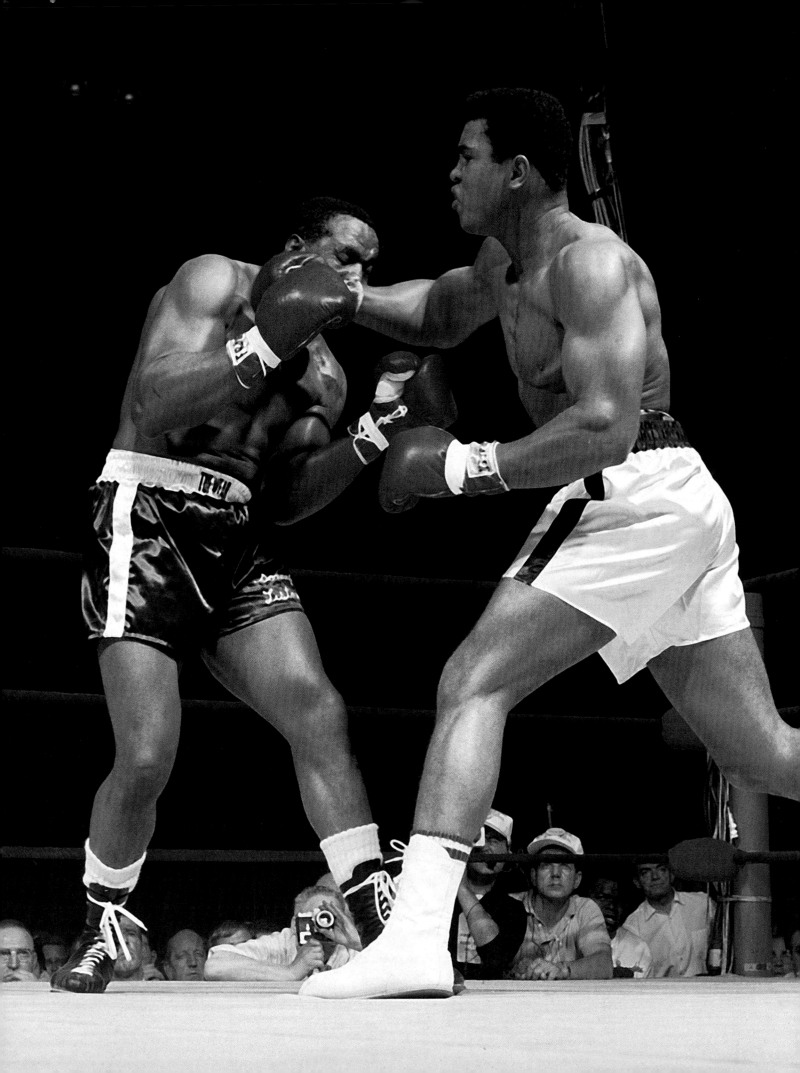

The maddest of existentialists, one of the great surrealists of our time, the king of all he sees, Ali had never before appeared so vulnerable and fragile, so pitiably unmajestic, so far from the universe he claims as his alone. He could barely hold his fork, and he lifted the food slowly up to his bottom lip, which had been scraped pink....

A couple of miles away in the bedroom of a villa, the man who had always demanded answers of Ali … lay in semidarkness.... His eyes were only slits, his face looked as if it had been painted by Goya. "Man, I hit him with punches that'd bring down the walls of a city," said [Joe] Frazier. Lawdy, Lawdy, he's a great champion."...

Time may well erode that long morning of drama in Manila, but for anyone who was there those faces will return again and again to evoke what it was like when two of the greatest heavyweights of any era met for a third time, and left millions limp around the world. Muhammad Ali caught the way it was: "It was like death. Closest thing to dyin' that I know of."

—MARK KRAM,
Oct. 13, 1975

stage, winning the world heavyweight title an unprecedented three times in his career (Evander Holyfield would equal this record in 1996). For almost two decades since his final retirement, in 1981, the boxing world has been desperately seeking "the next Ali," a search that is doomed to fail because there will never be another one like him. Of all the finest athletes of the 20th century, only Ali is universally known by the label he once so brazenly bestowed upon himself: the Greatest.   —*T.C.*

"With the exception of Martin Luther King, no black man in America had more influence than Ali during the years when Ali was in his prime."
—*THOMAS HAUSER, Ali biographer*

Two famed Ali opponents were Sonny Liston (opposite, left), who was floored in the first round in 1965 by the famous "Phantom Punch," and Joe Frazier (above, right), who lost by TKO in Round 15 after going toe-to-toe with Ali in the legendary "Thrilla in Manila" title fight.

Michael Jordan

In just his sixth NBA playoff game ever, on April 20, 1986, Michael Jordan scored 63 points at the Boston Garden against Larry Bird and the eventual league champion Celtics. After the game, Bird was asked to describe Jordan's performance, and he said, "I think he's God disguised as Michael Jordan."

How many times in Jordan's blessed career was he compared to Him? Perhaps the religious iconography exists because the classic image of No. 23 is "Air Jordan," a rocket-man flying amidst the ever-blossoming championship banners in the rafters at Chicago's United Center, soaring above the rest of the NBA like no player before him. Jordan obviously does not merit the capital 'H'—no one does—but the dude did play a divine game. And the absolute worship of Jordan is even more impressive because he is a sports contemporary. Unlike so many of the athletes of the earlier parts of this century, whose faults may be airbrushed away in the public's imagination, Jordan is very real. We have all had the opportunity to watch him

work on a daily basis, even to break him down to X's and O's on a telestrator, and no matter how hard we tried we could never find a flaw.

A check of his numbers is staggering. Jordan scored in double figures in 840 straight NBA games. His career scoring average of 31.5 points per game is the highest alltime, and he scored 50 points or more in 37 games. He produced 28 triple-doubles. Over the course of his 13-season career he won 10 NBA scoring titles, including a string of seven in a row broken only by his first retirement in 1993. He won five NBA most valuable player awards and, with his Bulls—and they were very much his—six league championships.

But Jordan was so much more than his ostentatious stats. No other athlete has ever possessed such a flair for the dramatic, such a knack for standing in the glaring spotlight of the postseason and delivering. It began when he was in college at North Carolina and was playing in the 1982 NCAA championship game against Georgetown. A mere freshman, Jordan nailed an 18-foot jump shot with 17 seconds left to win the national title. He never

The incomparable Jordan (opposite) led the Bulls to six titles during the 1990s, reinventing his playing style along the way.

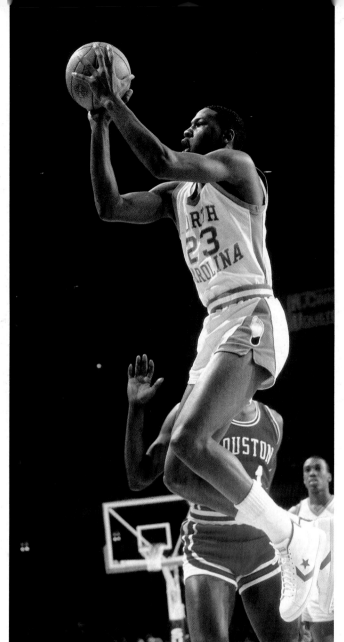

looked back. In the deciding game of a playoff series against Cleveland in 1989, he nailed a double-clutch jumper from the top of the key at the buzzer to steal a win. In Game 1 of the 1992 NBA Finals against Portland he scored 35 points in the first half, memorably retreating upcourt after sinking yet another three-pointer and shrugging his shoulders as if bemused by his own brilliance. As we were. Just five games after his return from his baseball sabbatical in 1995 he knocked down 55 points against the Knicks at Madison Square Garden and then sealed the victory with, of all things, an assist. In Game 5 of the 1997 Finals, weakened by a stomach ailment that made it difficult for him even to pull on his uniform, Jordan somehow scored a game-high 38 points, 15 of them in the final quarter, to silence the Jazz.

Jordan's famous protruding tongue might as well have been a gesture taunting the many frustrated contenders to his throne. It wasn't, of course, but in the '90s, Jordan didn't start a single basketball season that didn't end with a Bulls championship. He wouldn't allow anyone else to win. If he had to adjust

From his championship freshman year at North Carolina (above, left), to his third year with the Bulls (above, right), when he averaged 37.1 points per game, to the '93 NBA Finals (right), Jordan was the consummate winner.

"He is the most awesome player in the NBA. Today in Boston Garden, on national TV, in the playoffs, he put on one of the greatest shows of all time. I couldn't believe someone could do that against the Boston Celtics."

LARRY BIRD, after Jordan's 63-point performance against the Celtics on April 20, 1986

his style to win, so be it. He began his career as the jump-and-jam star of Michael Jordan's Flying Circus. Toward the end he preferred the shot that he had polished while playing pickup hoops games with his baseball teammates in Alabama, a magnificent fadeaway that made his opponents do just that. He reinvented himself with that shot in the latter stage of his career.

Jordan's effect spread way beyond the baselines. With him on their roster, the Bulls sold out home games for more than 10 years, and the waiting list for seasons tickets ballooned to 23,000 names. He received as many as 6,000 pieces of fan mail a month from all over the globe, and in his final season Jordan even signed a few pregame autographs—for the refs. During a stop in Atlanta on what would be his farewell tour, the

Spotlight

Michael Jordan's storybook sendoff in Game 6 of the 1998 NBA Finals is forever seared into the sporting collective consciousness: he drives forcefully on Utah defender Bryon Russell only to stop on a dime after two steps and, having created the space for himself (Russell stumbled trying to recover), knocks down the open 'J'. But the canonization of that moment shouldn't make us forget that Jordan's final flourish was not just a moment but an entire—dominant, almost transcendent—sequence, beginning with 41.9 seconds left. Utah's John Stockton had just made a three-pointer to give the Jazz an 86–83 lead. Jordan took the ball at the other

end and instantly scored, driving past Russell for a layup while burning only 4.8 seconds off the clock. Utah still led, 86–85, but on the baseline at the other end of the court Jordan sneaked up behind Karl Malone and stripped the ball out of his hands, then came back upcourt and sank his 17-footer over Russell. That gave Jordan 45 points for the night. The Jazz missed a final shot and the Bulls were champions yet again. Jordan had single-handedly taken over the game in the final minute, crushing the hopes of Jazz fans and providing himself with an unbeatable exit for his career. He would announce his retirement on Jan. 13, 1999.

Whether he was winning the slam-dunk contest at the 1988 All-Star Game (opposite), throwing down against the Sonics in the '96 regular season (above, right) or sailing to playoff victory against the Knicks in '93 (above, left), No. 23 proved that 'Air Jordan' was as good as his name.

Hawks drew a one-game NBA attendance record of 62,046 fans. Eight thousand of those seats had no view of the floor. Eight thousand people just wanted to say they'd been there whether they actually got to see Jordan or not. He hadn't even officially announced his retirement, but only hinted at it.

Jordan exploded just as the NBA exploded, and it's hard to decide which institution owed more to the other. Perhaps that will only be decided with time, when we see how much Jordan is missed. He had a huge influence on the NBA's television ratings and the cost of its broadcast rights, and his appeal extended to the wider marketplace as well. Advertisers urged consumers to Be Like Mike in their choice of everything from sneakers to breakfast cereal to batteries to french fries. His bald pate was so distinctive that he sold a line of cologne with no name or label on the package, just the silhouette of his head. *Fortune* magazine estimated that Jordan generated more than $10 billion for the world's economy. Heck, his rabid fans paid a total of $439 million to see him in a movie with Bugs Bunny.

Like Ali and Ruth, Jordan became an athlete unique to his era. As statesmen took a backseat to athletes and rock stars at the end of the 20th century, Jordan was arguably the most famous face on the globe. And no athlete has ever orchestrated a better curtain call to a career. With 5.2 seconds left in Game 6 of the 1998 NBA Finals and the Bulls trailing Utah by one point, Jordan faked his defender to the floor and drained the game- and series-winning jumper from the lane. He concluded the night with 45 points and his sixth NBA title. Jordan froze in his follow-through to that shot, holding the pose for a few beats as if he knew that he—and we—should savor it. At that glorious moment, who among us didn't want to be like Mike?   —*T.C.*

"Michael Jordan is the greatest basketball player ever. He was also the best player involved in a team sport of any kind. Of all the great players, he knew when to retire. And he was able to retire on top."

—*BOB KNIGHT,*
Indiana University
basketball coach

THE RECORD

YEAR	TEAM	G	FG %	FT %	REB	AST	PTS	PPG	RPG
1984-85	Chi	82	.515	.845	534	481	2313	28.2	6.5
1985-86	Chi	18	.457	.840	64	53	408	22.7	3.6
1986-87	Chi	82	.482	.857	430	377	3041	37.1	5.2
1987-88	Chi	82	.535	.841	449	485	2868	35.0	5.5
1988-89	Chi	81	.538	.850	652	650	2633	32.5	8.0
1989-90	Chi	82	.526	.848	565	519	2763	33.6	6.9
1990-91	Chi	82	.539	.851	492	453	2580	31.5	6.0
1991-92	Chi	80	.519	.832	511	489	2404	30.1	6.4
1992-93	Chi	78	.495	.837	522	428	2541	32.6	6.7
1994-95	Chi	17	.411	.801	117	90	457	26.9	6.9
1995-96	Chi	82	.495	.834	543	352	2491	30.4	6.6
1996-97	Chi	82	.486	.883	482	352	2431	29.6	5.9
1997-98	Chi	82	.465	.784	475	283	2357	28.7	5.8
TOTAL		930	.505	.838	5836	5012	29,277	31.5	6.3

Off the court, Jordan was just one of the guys (top); on it, he was anything but: Scottie Pippen aided the flu-ridden star after Jordan's heroic 38-point performance in Game 5 of the '97 NBA Finals (opposite), which led to the Bulls' fifth championship trophy (above, right).

Babe Ruth

The life of George Herman Ruth Jr. has always been problematic for those who teach the moral virtues. Beaten by his saloonkeeper father, Ruth was a rock-throwing truant and thief who, at age seven, was sent to a Baltimore reformatory, where he lived on and off until he was 19. The grown-up Ruth partook heroically of all the conventional vices and treated authority with disdain. He threw dirt in the eyes of umpires, missed curfews, feuded with managers, chased hecklers, swilled beer and went AWOL at the sight of a skirt—behavior which, had he not possessed a certain boyish charm and prodigious talent, would have made Ruth unemployable. And yet—and this is what confounds the moralists—Ruth is arguably the most accomplished and most beloved athlete of all time.

Even from the exit end of the century, it's easy to look back on Ruth's achievements and proclaim them unmatched. As a hitter he generated season and career home run numbers that transformed baseball forever and re-wired the circuitry of the American sports fan. As a pitcher he won 87 games in five seasons and set a World Series record for consecutive shutout innings (29⅔) that lasted more than 40 years. In 1921, Ruth hit 59 homers, drove in 171 runs, scored 177, walked 144 times and batted .378—impossible totals, for Ruth's time or any other. The year before, he produced a slugging percentage of .847. Seventy-nine years later, that record still stands.

It is far more difficult to fathom the man, to explain how a barrel-chested, spindly-legged libertine—"an inverted eggplant," as one writer described him—could perform feats beyond the dreams of the fit, the God-fearing and the disciplined. His biographer, Robert Creamer, saw this conundrum as the reason Ruth comes down to us as a cartoon, "a big, gluttonous slob who dropped out of a tree with a baseball bat in his hands." Look up "Ruthian" and you're likely to find the synonym "Bunyanesque." You're at the intersection of history and myth, and it might as well be Ruth striding alongside the giant blue ox named … Babe!

"He was the most uninhibited human being I have ever known," said John Debringer of *The New York Times*. "He just

One of a kind: Ruth (left) had the skills to dominate his era like no one before or since, and the charisma to become an **American** icon.

THE RECORD							
YEAR	TEAM	G	R	HR	RBI	SB	AVG
1914	Bos-A	5	1	0	2	0	.200
1915	Bos-A	42	16	4	21	0	.315
1916	Bos-A	67	18	3	15	0	.272
1917	Bos-A	52	14	2	12	0	.325
1918	Bos-A	95	50	11	66	6	.300
1919	Bos-A	130	103	29	114	7	.322
1920	NY-A	142	158	54	137	14	.376
1921	NY-A	152	177	59	171	17	.378
1922	NY-A	110	94	35	99	2	.315
1923	NY-A	152	151	41	131	17	.393
1924	NY-A	153	143	46	121	9	.378
1925	NY-A	98	61	25	66	2	.290
1926	NY-A	152	139	47	146	11	.372
1927	NY-A	151	158	60	164	7	.356
1928	NY-A	154	163	54	142	4	.323
1929	NY-A	135	121	46	154	5	.345
1930	NY-A	145	150	49	153	10	.359
1931	NY-A	145	149	46	163	5	.373
1932	NY-A	133	120	41	137	2	.341
1933	NY-A	137	97	34	103	4	.301
1934	NY-A	125	78	22	84	1	.288
1935	Bos-N	28	13	6	12	0	.181
TOTAL		2503	2174	714	2213	123	.342

did things." Visiting Ruth's hotel room one midnight, Ty Cobb found the Babe in bed smoking a cigar, with six club sandwiches, a platter of pig knuckles and a pitcher of beer arrayed before him. Cobb said the Bambino devoured the entire spread. Ruth's speech was similarly unbridled. Offered asparagus at a posh dinner party, he grinned and said, "Gee, I'd love some, lady, but asparagus turns my urine green."

But Ruth's profligacy was best expressed in home runs. He was still a pitcher when he hit 29 of them for the Boston Red Sox in 1919, 17 more dingers than anyone in either league. By age 26 he was already the career leader in homers. He hit 54 homers in 1920, and no one had hit more than 30 in a season before then.

As comfortable amid an adoring mob of schoolboys in Syracuse, N.Y. (opposite, top) as he was sliding in with another Yankee run (above) or belting one of his 2,873 career hits (inset, opposite), Ruth made the transition from Baltimore reformatory to national stardom with aplomb.

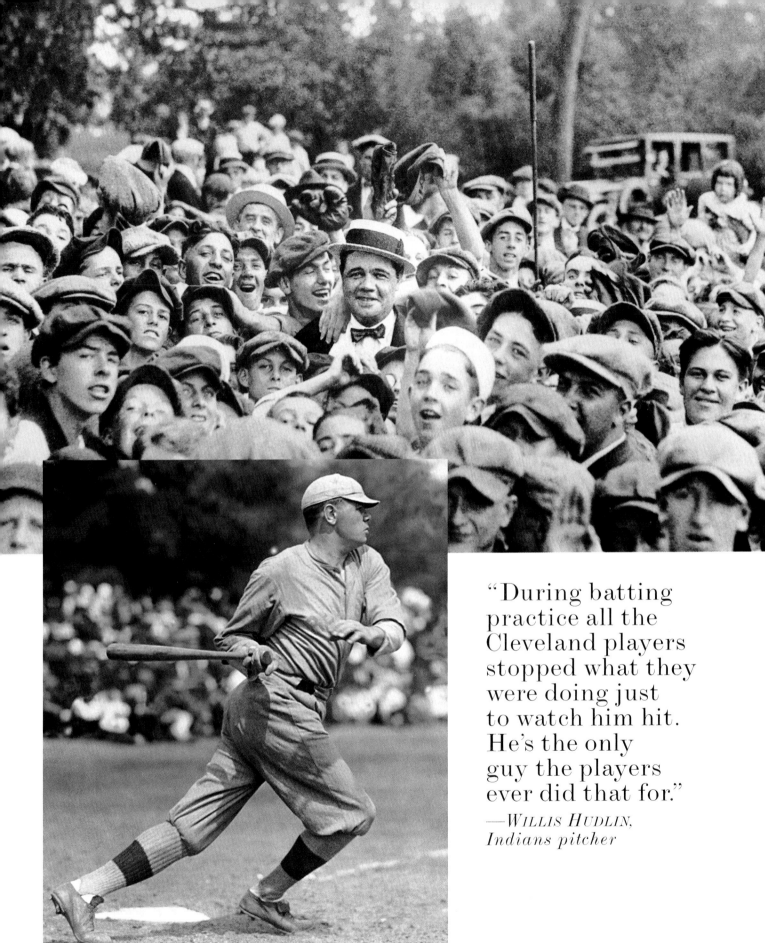

"During batting practice all the Cleveland players stopped what they were doing just to watch him hit. He's the only guy the players ever did that for."

—*WILLIS HUDLIN, Indians pitcher*

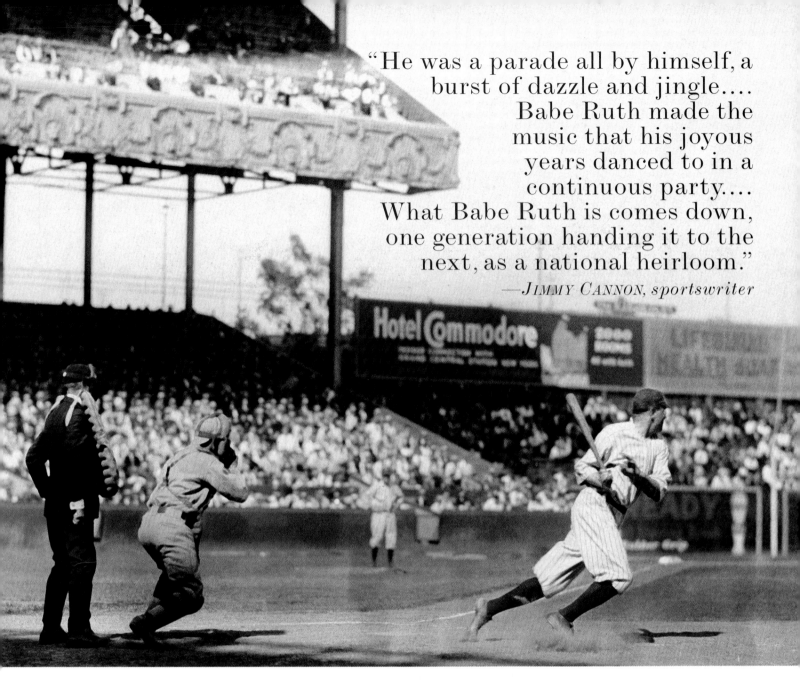

"He was a parade all by himself, a burst of dazzle and jingle.... Babe Ruth made the music that his joyous years danced to in a continuous party.... What Babe Ruth is comes down, one generation handing it to the next, as a national heirloom."
—JIMMY CANNON, *sportswriter*

Spotlight

The centerpiece of the Ruthian legend is undoubtedly the Called Shot in Game 3 of the 1932 World Series against the Chicago Cubs. There was bad blood between the Yanks and the Cubs for several reasons, among them that the Cubs had voted ex-Yankee shortstop Mark Koenig—who hit .353 during the Cubs' drive for the NL crown after being called up from the minors— only half a share of their postseason money. Before Game 1, Ruth called out to Koenig, "Hey Mark, who're these cheapskates you're with?"

The friction increased as the Yankees won Games 1 and 2 at home, 12–6 and 5–2, to take a 2–0 Series lead to Chicago, where the fans at Wrigley Field were ready for Ruth. He was booed lustily and had lemons thrown at him during batting practice, and when he came to bat in the fifth inning with the score tied 4–4, the crowd of 50,000 was roaring. Cubs players leaned out of the dugout to hurl insults at Ruth. He took two called strikes from Chicago pitcher Charlie Root, turning to the Cubs dugout after each

one and counting it off with his fingers. Root was furious at this display, and started jawing at Ruth.

What happened next is a matter of religious interpretation. The Babe either pointed at the pitcher or to the centerfield bleachers. (Some versions of the story have him pointing his bat at Root.) What happened after that, however, is exceedingly clear. Ruth walloped the longest home run ever seen at Wrigley Field, a tracer to the centerfield bleachers, where he may or may not have just pointed.

Rounding the bases, Ruth laughed out loud and clasped his hands over his head in triumph. Lou Gehrig was waiting for him at home plate, a broad smile lighting up his face. Only one newspaper reported specifically that Ruth had pointed at the centerfield fence, but that was all it took for the legend to take hold.

The forgotten coda to the story is that Lou Gehrig hit Root's very next pitch out of the park. The Yankees won the game 7–5 and swept the Series.

Ruth (opposite) and Lou Gehrig (above, left) were the heart of the Yankees' Murderer's Row order under manager John McGraw (above, shaking hands with Ruth) during the 1920s and '30s; they won four World Series together and in 1927 combined for 107 home runs and 339 RBIs.

"He made home run hitting look easy," said Shirley Povich of the *Washington Post*. "There was no violence in the stroke. He put everything into it, but he never looked like he was extending himself." In one six-year stretch with the Yankees that began in 1926, Ruth hit no fewer than 46 home runs a season and as many as 60—what Creamer called "the most sustained stretch of great hitting by any batter." Roger Maris, the man who broke Ruth's single-season home run record, hit more than 40 homers in a season only once in his career. Ruth did it 11 times. In 1927 he batted .356

and drove in 164 runs to go with his 60 homers.

They say that Ruth saved baseball by rescuing it from the Black Sox betting scandal of 1919. That, too, has to baffle the moralists. How could a boozy, cigar-puffing philanderer like Ruth restore a game's innocence?

To answer that question is to arrive at the conclusion *Sports Illustrated*'s Franz Lidz reached some years ago when he wrote, "Ruth was the superstar of the baseball little boys play." George Herman Ruth—denied a childhood of his own—simply chose not to grow up. —*J.G.*

Peerless Performers

Peerless Performers

While it is generally considered prudent never to say never, in the following chapter we believe we have rounded up a clique of athletes whose signature achievements will never be replicated. They have all set awesome standards, whether they be individual statistics, team championships or a dynamic combination of the two, that will never be observed again no matter how long their various sports are contested.

For instance, with the increasing emphasis on specialization across all of sports it is safe to say that no athlete will ever again attempt to be as accomplished at so many different activities as Jim Thorpe or Babe Didrikson.

Thorpe won gold medals in the pentathlon and decathlon at the 1912 Olympics in Stockholm, and later excelled in professional football and baseball. Didrikson won 17 straight golf tournaments in the 1940s, after taking two Olympic golds, in the javelin and hurdles, at the '32 Games in Los Angeles. Now that free agency has increased player transience, we will never see anyone in a major professional team sport win eight consecutive championships again, or 11 titles in 13 seasons with one club, as former Boston Celtics center Bill Russell did.

Other athletes in the following pages are simply floating in a statistical firmament that we can no longer imagine, in some cases because the face of their sport has changed or in others because the overall competition has improved dramatically. If Michael Jordan couldn't do it, then why would we expect anyone to equal Wilt Chamberlain's feats of 100 points in a single game, or a season scoring average of more than 50 points per game? In baseball these days, a player might rack up a .344 career average, or smack more than 500 career home runs, but no one will ever again do both, as Red Sox slugger Ted Williams did.

Golfer Jack Nicklaus won an astounding 20 majors, nine more than anybody else in the history of the game has won. Rod Laver cobbled together two Grand Slams, in 1962 and in '69, and in the three decades since we have witnessed only two other Slams by anybody, male or female. Wayne Gretzky produced the kind of mind-boggling NHL numbers in both goals and assists that won't be matched by your average two hockey Hall of Famers combined, and Pelé's 1,281 career goals are similarly stratospheric in the soccer world. Finally, who could imagine anybody else winning nine gold medals as both a sprinter and a long jumper over a span of four Olympics as the indomitable Carl Lewis has done?

Sports fans who witnessed the feats of these 10 marvelous athletes should consider themselves very fortunate, because generations to come will never see the likes of them again. Never.   —T.C.

The multi-talented Thorpe (above) and Williams (opposite) set sporting standards that will never be equaled.

Wilt Chamberlain

He was the first great hallucination of the age of televised sports. On a black-and-white screen, Wilt Chamberlain looked like an outsized stick figure, his massive biceps and thighs disguised by their elongation, his hands big enough to palm a medicine ball. Up close he was a man of impossible proportions, the waistband of his trunks riding at almost shoulder level on a 6'6" guard. "He was so large and so strong and his feats were so outlandish that he wouldn't be nicknamed for anything so mundane as a mere world, or planet, or star," wrote Ira Berkow of *The New York Times*. "He was named for an entire constellation. He was the Big Dipper."

So imposing a figure was Chamberlain that fans and writers worked overtime to cut him down. Wilt led the NBA in scoring seven times and in rebounding 11 times and was league MVP four times, but he also got booed regularly. He was unfairly defined by his principal weakness—those free throws that clanked off the rim at the rate of about five and a half per game—and by the undeniable fact that his Philadelphia Warriors of the early '60s couldn't beat the Boston Celtics, led by Chamberlain's nemesis, Bill Russell.

"Nobody roots for Goliath," said Wilt.

But nobody can deny that Chamberlain produced feats that shimmer in the record book like mirages on a desert road: his 100-point game against the Knicks on March 2, 1962; his 27.2 rebounds per game during the 1960–61 season; his 50.4 points-per-game average during the following season; his 55-rebound game in 1960 against—can this be right?—Russell and the Celtics. Not content to rewrite the record book, Chamberlain altered the rule book as well. In the 1950s, largely because of his impact, college officials banned offensive goaltending, over-the-backboard inbound passes and jumping from the foul line to dunk free throws. "I was just too big and too threatening," Chamberlain said when he was older.

The contemporaneous take on the Chamberlain-Russell rivalry was that Chamberlain was the greater athlete, while Russell, the unselfish defensive genius, was the better player. But when Wilt played on talented teams, such as the 1967 NBA champion Philadelphia 76ers or the 1972 champion Los Angeles Lakers, he was a team player

Chamberlain (opposite) was a new force in basketball—huge, intimidating and skilled—and his accomplishments were as outsized as his frame.

with unprecedented versatility. In 1968 he led the league in assists, with 702. He made the All-Defensive team in '72 and '73, and he led the league in shooting percentage nine times. "He never deserved his image," said Frank McGuire, who coached the supposedly uncoachable Chamberlain as a Warrior. "He was the best problem I ever had."

Chamberlain was similarly misjudged as a man. True, he was flamboyant and hedonistic. He drove sports cars at dangerous speeds, owned a Bel-Air mansion and boasted in his 1991 autobiography that he had enjoyed sex with 20,000 women in his lifetime. But Chamberlain never claimed he was the whole show. "You're only as good as the people you play against," he said after retirement. "I owe everything I have to Bill Russell and Walt Bellamy and Nate Thurmond. And the big guy from Cincinnati, Wayne Embry." His generosity didn't stop there. "I was the worst

Chamberlain was the tallest kid in his fourth-grade class (top), and that situation didn't change at Overbrook High School, where the rangy Chamberlain excelled as a quarter-miler (above), before moving on to the Universtiy of Kansas (opposite) to change college basketball forever.

"One day Wilt's going
to score 100 points.
Wait and see."
—AL ATTLES, a teammate of
Chamberlain's, February 1962

the Mountaintop

As tall as he was, it took Wilt
Chamberlain some time to reach
the heights. He was a past master of
individual accolades, leading the
league in scoring in his rookie season of 1959–60, when he averaged
37.6 points per game. Indeed, leading the NBA in scoring would
become routine for Chamberlain;
he did so in each of his first seven
seasons, and in his third he averaged
an amazing 50.4 points per game.
But Chamberlain developed almost
in lockstep with the rise of another
dominant force in the NBA, the
Boston Celtics, and so while Wilt
could produce numbers gaudier
than a Vegas casino, he couldn't get
a title in edgewise as the Celtics
reeled off eight straight from 1959
to '66.

That changed in 1967 when, not
coincidentally, Chamberlain changed
too. He concentrated on rebounding and defense and getting his
76ers teammates involved in the
offense. Second-year star Billy
Cunningham and veteran Chet
Walker each enjoyed career highs in
scoring as a result of Chamberlain's
largesse, and the Big Dipper averaged a none-too-shabby 24.1 points,
24.2 rebounds and 7.8 assists per
game. The Sixers jumped out to a
46–4 start and would not be
denied: After disposing of Boston in
the Eastern Division finals,
Philadelphia beat Wilt's old team,
the Warriors, four games to two for
the title. After eight years of regular-
season dominance, Wilt the Stilt had
finally made it to the top.

guy on the team, the Bob Uecker of the NBA," said Joe Ruklick, the former Northwestern All-America who fed Chamberlain on the bucket that brought Wilt his 100th point against the Knicks that night in 1962. "But Wilt made you feel like part of a family. He was quite a guy."

He was also quite an all-around athlete. Chamberlain was a star quarter-miler in high school, an outstanding high jumper in college, and a pro volleyball player after retiring from the NBA. The Kansas City Chiefs once considered hiring him to block field goals, and fight promoters came within an eyelash of giving him a bout with heavyweight champion Muhammad Ali.

The Greatest against the Big Dipper. Now that would have been huge. —*J.G.*

THE RECORD

YEAR	TEAM	G	FG %	FT %	REB	AST	PTS	PPG	RPG
1959-60	Phil	72	.461	.582	1941	168	2707	37.6	27.0
1960-61	Phil	79	.509	.504	2149	148	3333	38.4	27.2
1961-62	Phil	80	.506	.613	2052	192	4029	50.4	25.7
1962-63	S.F.	80	.528	.593	1946	275	3586	44.8	24.3
1963-64	S.F.	80	.524	.531	1787	403	2948	36.9	22.3
1964-65	S.F.-Phil	73	.510	.464	1673	250	2534	34.7	22.9
1965-66	Phil	79	.540	.513	1943	414	2649	33.5	24.6
1966-67	Phil	81	.683	.441	1957	630	1956	24.1	24.2
1967-68	Phil	82	.595	.380	1952	702	1992	24.3	23.8
1968-69	L.A.	81	.583	.446	1712	366	1664	20.5	21.1
1969-70	L.A.	12	.568	.446	221	49	328	27.3	18.4
1970-71	L.A.	82	.545	.538	1493	352	1696	20.7	18.2
1971-72	L.A.	82	.649	.422	1572	329	1213	14.8	19.2
1972-73	L.A.	82	.727	.510	1526	365	1084	13.2	18.6
TOTAL		**1045**	**.540**	**.511**	**23,924**	**4643**	**31,419**	**30.1**	**22.9**

Chamberlain's 76ers were tripped up in the 1968 playoffs by Boston and John Havlicek (above, No. 17), and his Lakers fell short against New York in the '73 NBA Finals (opposite), but Wilt won NBA championships in 1967 and '72, with the 76ers and the Lakers respectively.

"When Wilt Chamberlain
lifted me up and moved
me like a coffee cup so he
could get position."
—BOB LANIER, 6'10", 270-pound
former NBA center, on the most
memorable moment of his career

Babe Didrikson

Many sane people swear that Babe Didrikson once scored 99 points in a high school basketball game. Others insist she shot 91 on the very first day she swung a golf club. Or that she bowled 193 after just five minutes of instruction. Sports historian Frank G. Menke once compiled a statistic that as an amateur Didrikson entered 634 competitions and emerged victorious in 632 of them. None of this is true.

Yet it is enlightening. It's a testament to the incredible feats that Didrikson actually did accomplish that so many people believed these tall tales and even perpetuated them. It should also be noted that one of the primary lily gilders was Babe Didrikson.

She grew up a Texas tomboy in the 1920s, when a woman's place was in the kitchen. Mildred Didrikson fought hard to be an athlete because she simply could not suppress her gifted genes. As a young woman she didn't wear jewelry or makeup, nor did she own a pair of stockings or a girdle. For ignoring feminine conventions, she drew criticism and sometimes worse. Sportswriter Paul Gallico once wondered if Babe "should be addressed as Miss, Mrs., Mr. or It."

In fact, she was a modern incarnation of the mythical huntress Atalanta, who surpassed the athletic accomplishments of her male contemporaries and was shunned for it. A football player at her high school once offered his face and challenged Didrikson to take her best shot. She knocked him out cold. What else could she do? It took that kind of guts to embrace a nickname shared with Babe Ruth, the most renowned athlete on the planet.

Sure, Didrikson could cook and sew, but she also excelled at tennis, flyfishing, billiards, marbles, volleyball, swimming, rollerskating and gin rummy, and she could play some mean blues on the harmonica. And those were just her hobbies. Standing 5'5" and weighing only 125 pounds, she was an All-America basketball player in 1930, '31 and '32, regularly scoring 30 points in an era when entire teams were thrilled to score 20. She was an all-star softball player who also pitched for a barnstorming baseball team and once tossed a few spring training innings with the St. Louis Cardinals.

The Texas Tornado, as Babe was also nick-

Didrikson (left) did it all, from the javelin, in which she won a gold medal at the 1932 Olympics, to billiards, golf and even the harmonica.

> "Babe Didrikson was my idol. She was the one I wanted to be like ever since I read a story about her when I was a kid."
>
> —*Jackie Joyner-Kersee*

named, showed up at the women's national AAU track meet in 1932 and for three hours darted from one event to the next. She won the shot put, javelin, broad jump, baseball throw and 80-meter hurdles, and tied for first place in the high jump, scoring 30 points in all. The team in second place scored only 22 points and needed 22 athletes to do so.

En route to the 1932 Olympics in Los Angeles, Didrikson's train stopped briefly in Albuquerque, where she comandeered a Western Union bicycle and began pedaling around the platform hollering, "Ever heard of Babe Didrikson? You will! You will!" An inveterate braggart who was sometimes known to embellish her records or lie about her size and age to magnify her myth, Babe nevertheless backed up all of her Olympic boasts. First, she won the gold medal in the javelin and set the Olympic record. Then she shat-

Didrikson (inset) broke the tape and the world record in the 80-meter hurdles at the '32 Games (right), and she might have won a third gold medal in the high jump (top) had not a judges' decision that she used an illegal technique to clear the bar relegated her to the silver.

L P G A   R E C O R D

YEAR	EVENTS	BEST FINISH	EARNINGS	AVG
1950	10	I	$2,875	75.88
1951	14	I	$6,812	74.92
1952	8	I	$4,730	75.76
1953	10	I	$5,132	75.70
1954	17	I	$11,437	75.61
1955	8	I	$3,398	75.60

Won the U.S. Women's Open: 1948, 1950, 1954
Won Title Holders Championship: 1947, 1950, 1952
Won Western Open: 1940, 1944, 1945, 1950
Career Earnings: $66, 237

the Mountaintop

No one took the musical admonition "Climb every mountain" more seriously than Babe Didrikson. After ascending to Olympian heights with two gold medals at the 1932 Games in Los Angeles, Didrikson engaged in a bizarre vaudeville act to capitalize on her newfound fame. Decked out in a red, white and blue track suit, she ran a treadmill, hit plastic golf balls to the audience and played the harmonica. Later, she barnstormed for a season with the House of David baseball team.

But throughout these inanities, Didrikson was practicing for her next athletic ascent, in the world of professional golf. Her golfing mentor, Gene Sarazen, said he knew of only one golfer, Ben Hogan, who practiced more than Didrikson. Her hard work paid off as she won one of the first tournaments she entered, the 1935 Texas women's championship. But Didrikson was banned from entering any more amateur tournaments because of the money she earned from baseketball and baseball; at the time there were only two women's golf events open to professionals. Ever determined, she sat out three years to regain her amateur status and celebrated it on Jan. 21, 1943, by winning the California state championship. Five years later she won the U.S. Women's Open by eight strokes. After a 14-year climb, Didrikson had reached the top of another sporting mountain, and she didn't stop there. The following year she helped found the Ladies Professional Golf Association, and she would go on to win two more U.S. Opens.

> "Sometimes I find myself leaning back in a chair thinking about Babe, and I have to smile. She was the happiest girl you ever saw, like a kid."
> —*PATTY BERG, golfer*

tered the world record while winning the 80-meter hurdles. Finally, Didrikson tied teammate Jean Shirley in the high jump—both athletes broke the world record—but was forced to accept the silver medal when the judges decided that the technique on her final jump was illegal. Still, Tinseltown could hardly have written a better script for her, and after the Olympics Didrikson was one of the most celebrated athletes in America.

Looking for a new challenge, she eventually turned to golf. With the great Gene Sarazen as her mentor, Didrikson won 82 amateur and pro tournaments in her career, including an unprecedented string of 17 straight in 1946–47. Only 15 months after surgery for cancer that would take her life in 1956 at age 45, she won the 1954 U.S. Women's Open by a record 12 shots.

Yes, even the true stories of Babe Didrikson begin to sound like legends. No wonder lots of folks could never tell the difference.   —*T.C.*

Didrikson was a three-time All-America in basketball (above), and after her Olympic track and field glory, she turned to golf (left), and won 82 tournaments, including 17 straight in 1946–47; she was also a co-founder of the Ladies Professional Golf Association.

Wayne Gretzky

Wayne Gretzky possessed 61 NHL records when he retired, 62 if you count the record for most records. If the gaudy margins by which he holds many of those marks are any indication, they may as well etch a few of them in stone because nobody will ever surpass them or the man who spent 21 years in professional hockey living up to a nickname he got as a nine-year-old.

The Great One scored 2,857 points in his NHL career, 1,000 more than his closest competitor, Gordie Howe. In fact, Gretzky has more assists (1,963) than any other player in NHL history has *points*. Ponder the ridiculousness of that for a moment. If you took away all of Gretzky's goals—and with 894, he has more of them than anyone who has or probably ever will play the game—he would still be the leading point-getter in league history. He holds the career and single-season NHL records for points, goals and assists, and along the way he won nine Hart Trophies as the league MVP, three more than any other athlete in the NHL, NBA, NFL or Major League Baseball.

Gretzky accomplished all of this despite the fact that he was not the fastest skater or the strongest checker, nor did he have the most wicked shot. What he had was uncanny anticipation and vision and the quickest hockey mind of all time. He somehow knew where the puck was going long before it ever got there. He also possessed graceful moves that allowed him to steer clear of brawny defensemen, who rarely took cheap shots at Gretzky out of respect for his skill and in recognition of his importance to the NHL.

A precocious player at every level of the game, Gretzky played on a team of 10-year-olds when he was five. At age 16 he was the leading scorer in the World Junior Championships, despite being the youngest player in the event. At 17, he was the youngest player in the World Hockey Association, yet he made the All-Star game, where he was honored to skate on the same line with the aging Howe.

By that time Gretzky had made the definitive sweater No. 99 his, as a tribute to his boyhood idol, Howe, who wore No. 9. And Gretzky wasted no time making his unique number famous. When he shifted to the NHL in 1979, some skeptics thought that his slight build would be a liability in that extremely

Without great strength, speed or size, Gretzky (opposite) used his uncanny vision and preternatural passing skills to thoroughly dominate hockey.

> "The idea that Wayne is the player he is because of how hard he worked is garbage. What he does on the ice isn't taught; it comes straight down from the Lord."
> —GLEN SATHER

THE RECORD

YEAR	TEAM	GP	G	A	PTS
1979-80	Edm	79	51	86	137
1980-81	Edm	80	55	109	164
1981-82	Edm	80	92	120	212
1982-83	Edm	80	71	125	196
1983-84	Edm	74	87	118	205
1984-85	Edm	80	73	135	208
1985-86	Edm	80	52	163	215
1986-87	Edm	79	62	121	183
1987-88	Edm	64	40	109	149
1988-89	LA	78	54	114	168
1989-90	LA	73	40	102	142
1990-91	LA	78	41	122	163
1991-92	LA	74	31	90	121
1992-93	LA	45	16	49	65
1993-94	LA	81	38	92	130
1994-95	LA	48	11	37	48
1995-96	LA-StL	80	23	79	102
1996-97	NYR	82	25	72	97
1997-98	NYR	82	23	67	90
1998-99	NYR	70	9	53	62
TOTAL		**1487**	**894**	**1963**	**2857**

by scoring 92 goals and making 120 assists for a 212-point season. It's difficult to say which is the centerpiece to Gretzky's extraordinary career, that year or the 1985–86 season, when he racked up an astonishing 163 assists and an NHL-record 215 points. Gretzky himself would probably pick another year, since Edmonton fell short of the Stanley Cup each of those seasons. While no other player has ever scored 200 points in a season, Gretzky *averaged* 203 per season over the six-year span from 1981–82 to '86–87.

But make no mistake, Gretzky was about more than garish numbers. His teams won championships. In 1983–84 he guided the young and talented Oilers to their first Stanley Cup, scoring twice in the Game 5 clincher that dethroned the four-time defending champion New York Islanders. The following season the Oilers defeated Philadelphia in the finals in a symbolic triumph of finesse over power. Gretzky won the Conn Smythe trophy as MVP of the playoffs. Edmonton would cap-

physical era of the league, but Gretzky won the Hart trophy in the Edmonton Oilers' debut season in the league. The next season he broke Phil Esposito's NHL record for points with 164. In his third season he achieved the magical mark of 50 goals in 50 games with room to spare: he scored his 50th in the 39th game of the year. All of that was a prelude to 1981–82, when Gretzky redefined the limits

Gretzky's shot (above) was not overpowering, yet it found the net an NHL-record 894 times, and while his knack for scoring goals waned in the later stages of his career, he never lost his deft passing touch, leading the league in assists five times with the Los Angeles Kings (opposite).

"It took me about two days to see how special he was. This is not an ordinary superstar we're talking about. This is the greatest player ever to put on a pair of skates."
—*LEE FOGOLIN, former Gretzky teammate*

the NHL's decision to place expansion franchises in non-traditional locales like Tampa, Fla., and Nashville. But that was by no means Gretzky's only purpose in L.A.: He guided the Kings to the Stanley Cup finals in 1993.

After a stint in St. Louis, Gretzky would finish his unparalleled NHL career with the New York Rangers, and toward the end of his final season he knocked down the only barrier left before him. On March 29, 1999, he scored the 1,072nd goal of his professional career to break Howe's record of 1,071 (the WHA statistics of both men are included in those totals). Just before the Great One skated his Last One, on April 18, 1999, the league announced that his No. 99 jersey would be retired by every NHL team. Hockey's highest number will forever belong to Gretzky. It's likely that hockey's highest numbers will, too.   —*T.C.*

ture two more Cups in the next three seasons.

In August 1988, a month after his gala wedding to actress Janet Jones, Gretzky was exported from Canada to Hollywood in the most stunning trade in NHL history. Los Angeles was hardly a hockey hotbed at the time, but Gretzky was an ideal ambassador for the game. He spread the NHL gospel to the unlikely climes of Southern California and figured prominently in

the Mountaintop

By the time Wayne Gretzky began his fifth season in the NHL, he had already made his mark in league history. He had scored 92 goals in the 1981–82 season, a record whose lifespan will be measured in geologic time, and the following year he averaged an unprecedented 1.56 assists per game. But he and his Edmonton Oilers had yet to win a championship. Gretzky knew that if

he didn't get his name on Lord Stanley's cup, all of his stratospheric scoring records, the Everest-size piles of assists, would provide cold comfort in his dotage.

In '82–83, after leading the league in scoring and winning the MVP award for the fourth consecutive year, Gretzky guided the Oilers to their first Stanley Cup finals. They were unceremoniously swept by the

three-time incumbent New York Islanders, and Gretzky was held to four assists and zero goals in the series. But the setback only made him resume his ascent in '83–84 with added fire. He scored at least one point in each of the first 51 games of that season, yet another of his records that may never be matched. He finished the year with his usual mind-boggling numbers—

87 goals, 118 assists—and the Oilers again met the Islanders in the finals. After splitting the first two games, the Oilers broke the series open with consecutive 7–2 routs and then wrapped it up with a 5–2 win. Gretzky scored two goals in Game 5 of the finals, sealing what he described as "my single biggest thrill in hockey." The Great One had summitted, his superstar status minted.

Gretzky will go into the Hall of Fame as an Oiler (above), having won three Stanley Cups with Edmonton, but he had his share of thrills with other teams, including Los Angeles, which he sent into the 1993 Stanley Cup finals with a series-winning goal, his third of the game (opposite).

Rod Laver

Rod Laver's muscular left arm was attached to a body so pale, thin and bowlegged that opponents wondered if his arm was the result of some secret Australian research program. In a sense, it was. He built up the arm when he was a teenager in Queensland by practicing wristy strokes until he ached from shoulder to forearm. "It's the basis of my game, spin," he said years later, after he had become the greatest tennis player in the world. "Spin keeps me excited."

His topspin backhand was the shot that got the most attention—it hit opponents' rackets like a bucket of water—but Laver also played dinks, chips, smashes, slices and evil drop shots that jumped back into the net before they could be returned. He was so good that in 1969, when he won his unprecedented second Grand Slam, *Sports Illustrated*'s Roy Blount Jr. wrote that "it looks as though the sport will have to be opened considerably wider, to include angels, highly trained kangaroos or something as yet unenvisaged, before anyone else will be in Laver's league."

The Rocket learned to play on his family's cattle ranch, trying to keep up with two older brothers on a homemade court of creek-bottom loam and red anthill crusts. He was taught the finer points of technique and tactics by Harry Hopman, the Australian Davis Cup captain, and by the time he was 18 Laver really was a rocket, winning junior championships in Australia, Canada and the U.S. He led Australian sweeps of the Davis Cup in 1960, '61 and '62, seized his first Wimbledon title and the No. 1 ranking in '61 and then won everything in '62—the Australian, French and U.S. Opens and Wimbledon—a feat previously accomplished only by Don Budge and Maureen Connolly.

Laver then turned professional, which in 1963 was tantamount to taking a vow of obscurity. The pros traveled like jazz bands, playing one-night stands in badly-lit venues with makeshift courts. Laver started his pro career horribly, losing regularly to top-ranked Ken Rosewall and formidable opponents like Lew Hoad, John Newcombe and Tony Roche. But he wasted little time elevating his game, and his successful toppling of Rosewall breathed new life into the pro circuit. "If he

What Laver (opposite) lacked in size—he was 5'8½" and weighed 155 pounds—he made up for with superb range and a stunning variety of shots.

Sports Illustrated's Roy Blount Jr. pointed out that the 1969 U.S. Open, in which men's singles champion Rod Laver earned $16,000, was the "richest tennis tournament ever." Ruefully describing the advances of capitalism in tennis, he lamented, among other things, "the fact that a can of domestic beer set you back 75¢." Such complaints seem positively quaint as we approach the year 2000, when *ballboys* probably earn close to $16,000 for their efforts at the U.S. Open, and players, well, their earnings are as out-of-sight as center court is from the top row of the new Arthur Ashe Stadium.

But Blount was absolutely right about the '69 U.S. Open, and in more ways than one. In the nascent era of open tennis, the '69 U.S. Open was the richest tournament to date in strictly economic terms, and to Rocket Rod Laver, it was priceless. It completed his second Grand Slam sweep of all four majors and permanently placed him in the tennis pantheon. When Laver won his first Grand Slam in 1962 it was mightily impressive—Don Budge was the only man to accomplish the feat before him—but his second Slam is the "Grandest Slam," as Blount called the triumph, because it was the first achieved in the open era. And it hasn't been done since in men's tennis. Laver outlasted a heavy downpour and Arthur Ashe in a tense semifinal and then dispatched fellow Australian Tony Roche 7–9, 6–1, 6–2, 6–2 in the final to claim his rare prize—genuine consideration as the greatest tennis player of all time.

hadn't joined us," said Hoad, "we might just as well have called it quits."

The approval of open tennis in 1968 gave Laver the opportunity to better Budge and Connolly. He did so in 1969, capping his Slam reprise with a win at rain-soaked Forest Hills, where helicopters hovered overhead to dry the courts. "It's those wristy strokes of his that win," said Rosewall. "He has so much power in his left forearm that it obviously

gives him a feeling of strength and confidence to play those unorthodox shots."

Despite Laver's appearance—writers were forever comparing him to small animals or a pterodactyl, lavishing particular attention on his beaked nose and freckled skin—he was, ounce for ounce, the match of any athlete in the world. His 155-pound body was as hard as cobblestone, and he moved so quickly that he made his side of

THE RECORD				
MAJOR TITLES				
YEAR	AUS	FRENCH	WIMB	U.S.
	S-D-M	S-D-M	S-D-M	S-D-M
1959	0-1-0	0-0-0	0-0-1	0-0-0
1960	1-1-0	0-0-0	0-0-1	0-0-0
1961	0-1-0	0-1-1	1-0-0	0-0-0
1962	1-0-0	1-0-0	1-0-0	1-0-0
1963	0-0-0	0-0-0	0-0-0	0-0-0
1964	0-0-0	0-0-0	0-0-0	0-0-0
1965	0-0-0	0-0-0	0-0-0	0-0-0
1966	0-0-0	0-0-0	0-0-0	0-0-0
1967	0-0-0	0-0-0	0-0-0	0-0-0
1968	0-0-0	0-0-0	1-0-0	0-0-0
1969	1-1-0	1-0-0	1-0-0	1-0-0
1970	0-0-0	0-0-0	0-0-0	0-0-0
1971	0-0-0	0-0-0	0-1-0	0-0-0
TOTAL	3-4-0	2-1-1	4-1-2	2-0-0

"When he is in a tough spot, Laver doesn't in any way retreat. He gets bolder and bolder and uses his wide range of shots without fear. He has sheer bravery and a beautiful sense of play."

—C.M. JONES, *tennis writer*

Still an amateur, Laver (above, right) defeated Roy Emerson (above, left) at Forest Hills to complete his first Grand Slam in 1962; as a professional, he downed Tony Roche at the U.S. Open in 1969 (opposite) to claim his historic second Slam.

"He's exceptional, he's unorthodox and he's someone you couldn't copy. As a champion, his performances and court temperament could be held up as a fine model for young players. But his playing style certainly couldn't be, because he has shots that few other players can produce."
—*KEN ROSEWALL, on Laver*

the court look as cramped as a train vestibule. Off the court he was a surprisingly shy man who bit his fingernails. On the court he was a Torquemada, glaring at opponents with pitiless eyes—"steel beads looking out of an ice box," in the words of SI's John Underwood.

But Laver was never a showman. He said,

"I talk to myself a little bit and throw a racket occasionally, but I don't perform at the expense of winning. Are you more popular if you're outspoken? Are you less popular if your color is the same through life, instead of red one minute and blue the next?"

Laver's spin on life, as with his shots, was sometimes hard to pick up.   —*J.G.*

At Wimbledon in 1969 (opposite and above) the scrappy Laver chased down impossible shots and slammed winners with authority en route to his 6–4, 5–7, 6–4, 6–4 victory over fellow Australian John Newcombe in the final.

Carl Lewis

He was a fop. He was a dandy. When he wasn't racing, the world's fastest man wore red leather pullovers with see-through slits and dangling zippers. He collected china and crystal, carried a makeup bag and cut his hair in a stylized high fade. "People aren't what they wish they were," said his outspoken sister, Carol. "And we are."

But running fast was never Carl Lewis's goal in life. He wanted to fly. Had he been born a hundred years earlier, he probably would have been one of those daredevil inventors in the old films, the fellows flapping balsa-wood wings. As it happened, he took up the long jump and did his flying off a tartan runway, out to the farthest reaches of a sandpit.

To jump far—to jump, say, 28 feet—Lewis transformed his sprinter's body into a biogyro, windmilling his right arm while pumping his legs for momentum and balance. But the key to long jumping is speed. When Lewis hit the takeoff board, after covering 146' 6" in 21 explosive strides, he needed to be traveling at nearly 27 mph—fast enough

Lewis (right), who retired with nine Olympic gold medals, won the second of a record-tying four consecutive golds in the long jump at Seoul in 1988.

THE RECORD

OLYMPICS

YEAR	SITE	EVENT	FINISH	TIME/DIST.
1984	Los Angeles	100 Meters	First	9.99
1984	Los Angeles	200 Meters	First	19.80 (OR)
1984	Los Angeles	Long Jump	First	28 ft. ¼ in.
1984	Los Angeles	4 x 100 Relay	First	37.83 (WR)
1988	Seoul	100 Meters	First	9.92 (OR)
1988	Seoul	200 Meters	Second	19.79
1988	Seoul	Long Jump	First	28 ft. 7¼ in.
1992	Barcelona	Long Jump	First	28 ft. 5½ in.
1992	Barcelona	4 x 100 Relay	First	37.40 (WR)
1996	Atlanta	Long Jump	First	27 ft. 10¾ in.

WORLD CHAMPIONSHIPS

YEAR	SITE	EVENT	FINISH	TIME/DIST.
1983	Helsinki	100 Meters	First	10.07
1983	Helsinki	Long Jump	First	28 ft. ¾ in.
1983	Helsinki	4 x 100 Relay	First	37.86
1987	Rome	100 Meters	First	9.93 (WR)
1987	Rome	Long Jump	First	28 ft. 5¼ in.
1987	Rome	4 x 100 Relay	First	37.90
1991	Tokyo	100 Meters	First	9.86 (WR)
1991	Tokyo	4 x 100 Relay	First	37.50 (WR)

OR=Olympic record; WR=world record

to be ticketed in a school zone. "Jumping is all a matter of careful preparation," he said, and the biggest part of his preparation was speed training.

That dovetailed nicely with Lewis's other pursuits on the track, the 100- and 200-meter dashes. At the 1984 Olympics in Los Angeles, Lewis won the long jump, the 100 and the 200, and he anchored the gold medal–winning 4 x 100-meter relay team to match Jesse Owens's historic four-gold performance at Berlin in 1936. If not for a faulty baton pass and a feisty training partner, Lewis might have repeated that feat at Seoul in the 1988 Olympics. He won the 100 after Canada's Ben Johnson was infamously disqualified for steroid use, and he became the second repeat winner in the history of the Olympic long

jump, leaping 28'7½". But Lewis was edged in the 200 by his young training partner Joe DeLoach, and the U.S. 4 x 100-meter relay team was disqualified for a faulty baton pass.

Three years later, at age 30, Lewis was a part of the fastest 100-meter field in history. The fastest part. As six men in the field broke 10 seconds, an event unequaled before or since, Lewis clocked a world-record 9.86 seconds. A year after that, at the Barcelona Olympics, he won his third gold in the long jump and anchored a world-record time in the 4 x 100. No one could deny that Lewis was the greatest athlete in U.S. track and field history.

But popularity, it seemed, could be denied him. Adored in Europe, where track is more popular, Lewis foundered at home. Americans called him a prima donna, remembering his refusal to try for a world-record long jump after he had secured the gold in Los Angeles (He was, not unreasonably, saving his strength for the 200.) They chafed at his vanity, his smugness. Aiming to please, Lewis had his nose re-shaped, put on eyeliner, wore outlandish outfits and recorded a pop song called "He's a Star." But fans didn't like his act at the '91 World Championships, where Lewis sulked after Mike Powell cracked Bob Beamon's 23-year-old long-jump record.

"Many tried to rip me," Lewis has said, "break me down over money, over being gay." Lewis insists that he isn't gay—just flashy, as befits a star. He said, "It's not as though six people have caught me in bed with six men."

His performance in the 1996 Olympics defied the conventional belief that athletes with fast-twitch muscles—sprinters, leapers—are done by 30, and attached a perhaps appropriately mixed ending to his Olympic career. Thirty-five years old and a long shot to even

"Carl proved tonight what he proves every time he gets into the blocks, every time he steps onto a long-jump runway, every time he steps onto the track for a relay race—that he's the greatest track athlete ever."
—DENNIS MITCHELL, *after Lewis's world record 9.86 100-meter dash at the 1991 world championships*

At the Los Angeles Games in 1984, Lewis (opposite) duplicated Jesse Owens's famous quadruple triumph at Berlin in 1936, winning the 100-meter dash, the 200-meter dash and the long jump (above) and anchoring the winning 4x100-meter relay team.

reach the Olympics—he qualified at the trials by a mere inch—Lewis leaped 27' 10¾" in Atlanta to win yet another gold medal, matching discus thrower Al Oerter's track and field record of four consecutive Olympic golds in the same event. The medal was Lewis's ninth, which tied him with three other athletes for the second-most Olympic gold medals. *People* magazine punned, "Just Like Gold Times." Yet Lewis cast a shadow over this crowning glory by openly campaigning to be added to the 4 x 100-meter relay team so that he would have a chance at a 10th gold medal and thus tie Ray Ewry as the Olympic athlete with the most golds. Lewis had not qualified for the event, and if he had been added, it would have meant dropping another athlete.

Flamboyant and provocative to the end, Lewis said, "I always knew that whatever people thought of me, the root of my problem was in my sport," he said. "But I have no bitterness. They had their own idea about what was good for track."

His controversial comments aside, Lewis had undoubtedly been good—very good—for track in his unsurpassed 18-year career.   —*J.G.*

Lewis won the adoration of fans at the 1983 world championships in Helsinki (opposite), where he captured three gold medals, and at the 1992 Olympics in Barcelona, where he brought home the United States' 4x100-meter relay team in world-record time (above).

"He sent a message. You better train hard 'cause Carl ain't joking."
—JOHN DRUMMOND, *sprinter*

It wasn't supposed to happen. It couldn't have happened. But the man who made the U.S. Olympic team by a mere inch, the man who made it to the finals only by grabbing onto the last handrail on the last caboose, the oldest man in the field won the gold with ancient legs, gray hair and a heart that stays forever young.

Carl Lewis beat age, gravity, history, logic and the world on Monday night at a rocking Olympic Stadium in Atlanta to win the gold medal in the long jump, becoming the only track and field athlete besides the discus thrower Al Oerter to win four gold medals in a single event. It was his fourth and last Olympics, his ninth gold, his 10th medal and quite possibly his most impossible moment in an impossibly brilliant career.

... You try to give the man a gold watch, and he steals your gold medal instead. You ask him to pass the torch, and he sets your Olympics on fire instead. "You've just seen a great performer at the end of his career," said Lewis's coach, Tom Tellez. "People thought he couldn't do it, but he did. He's the greatest athlete I've ever seen."

... And when they called him forward to his last Olympic victory stand in that sweet Georgia night, he covered his face with his hands again and again, as if even he couldn't believe this. And before they played the first note, he was crying again.

Boy, some guys just can't stand happy endings.

—RICK REILLY
Aug. 5, 1996

Jack Nicklaus

When Bobby Jones said of Jack Nicklaus,"He plays a game with which I am not familiar," he did not choose his words lightly. The young Nicklaus conquered traditional golf courses the way a seven-foot-tall mountain climber would ascend Mt. Rainier: using footholds and handholds that have never been touched. Nicklaus's tee shots sailed over the established choke points of fairway bunkers and lateral water hazards. His irons flew high and landed softly. From the rough Nicklaus was unmatched, a Bunyanesque excavator of glory where others found only more grief. "He may be the greatest world athlete of the last quarter-century," Tom Boswell wrote in 1987. "At the least he's the person in sports most worthy of study if the subject that fascinates you most is the source of excellence."

Nicklaus's athletic gifts were so unmistakable that it took years for golf fans to recognize that his greatest edge was his strategic mind. If Arnold Palmer was the visceral attacker of golf courses, Nicklaus was the methodical deconstructionist, weighing his shot options with actuarial precision. To watch Nicklaus putt was to watch a diamond cutter at work—three minutes of scrutiny and analysis followed by a single, sure stroke that resulted in something sparkling. Course management was his religion, the considered shot his rite. "The Nicklaus of the '60s and '70s was head and shoulders above everybody else," *Sports Illustrated*'s Rick Reilly wrote in 1994, "but mostly head."

While growing up in Columbus, Ohio, in the '50s, young Jack learned the game on the silky fairways of Scioto Country Club. To teach him how to turn around a stable spine, Scioto's head pro, Jack Grout, held the young Nicklaus's head while he swung. In later years, Nicklaus remained so centered and unshakable that his name on a leader board was enough to send challengers spinning into bogeyland. He won the first of his 18 major championships, the 1962 U.S. Open at Oakmont, when he was 22, and the last, the 1986 Masters, when he was 46. During that span, in which he also recorded an astonishing 19 second-place finishes in majors, Nicklaus never blew a title. The ones he lost—most notably his unforgettable duels with Tom

Nicklaus (opposite) possessed such prodigious physical talents that his greatest asset, course management, went unrecognized for a time.

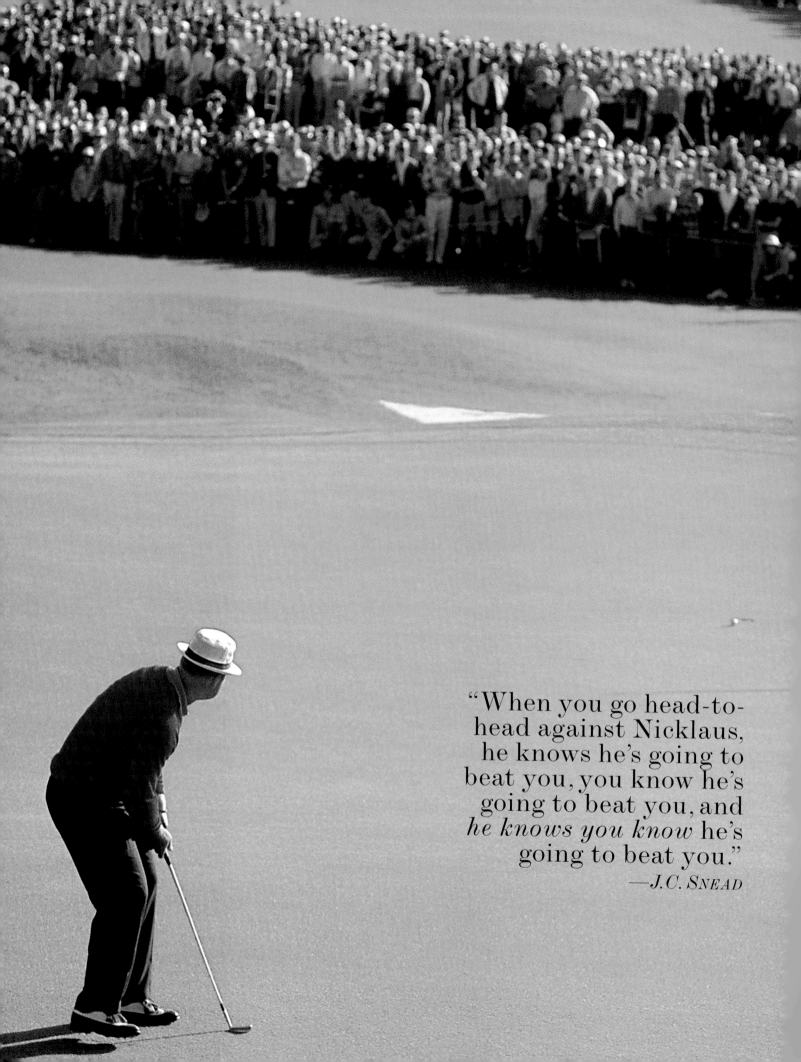

"When you go head-to-head against Nicklaus, he knows he's going to beat you, you know he's going to beat you, and *he knows you know* he's going to beat you."
—*J.C. SNEAD*

Augusta National officials had
declared Tuesday to be Jack
Nicklaus Day, but somehow he
heard *week*. They dedicated a plaque
to him on a drinking fountain near
the 16th green, and he even cried.
But the problem was he didn't
understand the Augusta National
Plaque Policy, which is that when
you get one, it means you're long
since done, you're toast, you're the
toast being toasted, and you're supposed to shake everybody's hand,
shoot 79-81–160 and disappear, like
a good little legend....
If Nicklaus had sunk just a few
more putts on Sunday, he'd be your
Masters champion right now, and
you might still be trying to get your
father down from the roof. A birdie
left on the lip at 8. A bunny missed
by an inch at 9. He wound up losing
by four to the winner, Mark
O'Meara, who had 10 fewer putts
and hit 10 fewer greens. Nobody's
been this old and straight since
Lawrence Welk. As it was, Nicklaus
finished sixth, whipped all four 1997
majors champions, became the oldest man to finish in the top 10 at
the Masters and reminded us all
how nice it would be if he never
went away at all.

—RICK REILLY
April 20, 1998

Watson at Turnberry in 1977 and Pebble
Beach in '82—were examples of someone
playing his best to beat the best. "If you
wanted to win the [U.S.] Open," SI's Walter
Bingham recalls, "you had to get by Nick-
laus. Arnold Palmer, Lee Trevino and Tom
Watson won four Opens among them, and
Nicklaus was second in them all."

As great as he was at holing out, Nicklaus
was even greater at reinventing himself. He won
his two U.S. Amateur championships, in 1959
and '61, with a boot camp haircut, a beefy body

and a stormy brow that gave him the look of a
renegade military policeman. A decade later, he
roamed courses with soft bangs, a slimmer body
and a gracious smile—a makeover as dramatic
as his switch from baggy khakis to gaudy poly-
ester slacks. When he won the '86 Masters,
the Golden Bear strolled through the golden
afternoon sunlight of Augusta National, with
the loudest roars ever heard on a golf course
echoing in the pines around him.

What Nicklaus understood, and what most
golfers never learn, is that golf is a game that

**Palmer looked over Nicklaus's shoulder during the U.S. victory in the 1971 Ryder Cup (above), but in golf history it was the other way
around, as Nicklaus's 1966 Masters title (opposite), his second in a row and third in four years, confirmed that he was Palmer's heir apparent.**

"Nicklaus has the remarkable combination of power and finesse, and he is one of the smartest guys ever to walk the fairways. And he has been an extraordinary leader. What more is there to say? Jack Nicklaus is the greatest competitor of them all."
—GENE SARAZEN

must be constantly re-learned. "The game is most fun when you are experimenting," he said at 40, when he was taking short-game lessons from Phil Rodgers. "I probably have forgotten more about golf than I will ever learn. What you do is remember some of the things you thought you'd never forget."

Nicklaus was proof that memory, if heeded, could sustain performance. In 1998, at age 58 and in need of reconstructive hip surgery, he made the Sunday turn at the Masters only two strokes off the lead. And while he did not win—Mark O'Meara did—for a couple of hours the greatest golfer in history walked out of his time and beyond reason, causing sportswriters to tremble and old men to rub their eyes. When Nicklaus drove the ball 330 yards on the ninth hole, two-time U.S. Open champion Ernie Els shook his head in disbelief.

Nicklaus just smiled. He was playing, one last time, the game he had made familiar to us all.
—J.G.

Nicklaus finished second to Tom Watson in the 1982 U.S. Open at Pebble Beach (above), but in 1986, at age 46, he won the Masters a record sixth time (opposite, left) before shifting predominantly to the Senior tour (opposite, right) in 1990.

THE RECORD

YEAR	EVENTS	SCORING AVG.	1ST	2ND	3RD	EARNINGS($)
1962	26	70.80	3	3	4	61,868
1963	25	70.42	5	2	3	100,040
1964	26	69.96	4	6	3	113,284
1965	24	70.09	5	4	2	140,752
1966	19	70.58	3	3	3	111,419
1967	23	70.23	5	2	3	188,998
1968	22	69.97	2	3	1	155,285
1969	23	71.06	3	1	0	140,167
1970	19	70.75	2	3	2	142,149
1971	18	70.08	5	3	3	244,490
1972	19	70.23	7	3	0	320,542
1973	18	69.81	7	1	1	308,362
1974	18	70.06	2	3	0	238,178
1975	16	69.87	5	1	3	298,149
1976	16	70.17	2	2	1	266,438
1977	18	70.36	3	2	1	284,509
1978	15	71.07	3	2	0	256,672
1979	12	72.49	0	0	1	59,434
1980	13	70.86	2	1	0	172,386
1981	16	70.70	0	3	0	178,213
1982	15	70.90	1	3	2	232,645
1983	16	70.88	0	3	1	256,158
1984	13	70.75	1	2	1	272,595
1985	15	71.81	0	2	1	165,456
1986	15	71.56	1	0	0	226,015
1987	11	72.89	0	0	0	64,686
1988	9	72.78	0	0	0	28,845
1989	10	72.35	0	0	0	96,594
1990*	4	68.60	2	1	1	350,000
1991*	5	69.79	3	0	0	343,734
1992*	4	71.00	0	1	1	114,547
1993*	6	71.00	1	0	0	206,028
1994*	6	70.35	1	0	0	239,278
1995*	7	69.68	1	2	1	538,800
1996*	7	70.92	2	1	0	360,861
1997*	6	71.41	0	1	0	239,932

Note: Official tour events only. *Senior Tour results.

Pelé

Few Americans know his real name. Most just assume it is Pelé, when in fact that is a mysterious moniker assigned to him by other children when he was eight years old, playing soccer barefoot in the streets of Brazil. His given name is actually Edson Arantes do Nascimento. Edson as in Thomas. Thomas Edison.

Granted, Pelé did not invent soccer, but with his light-bulb brilliance and ingenuity, he perfected it. When he signed his first pro contract at age 15, the man who brought him onto the Brazilian club Santos, Valdemar de Brito, reportedly said, "This boy will be the greatest soccer player in the world." Pelé scored four goals in his first league game for Santos, and two years later—at age 17—scored two goals in Brazil's 5–2 victory over Sweden in the World Cup final. By the time Brazil won another World Cup in '62, Pelé was widely acknowledged as the world's best player in the world's most popular sport.

For an athlete never permitted to use his hands, Pelé's reach proved immense. If you took a poll of sports fans around the world, would a Ugandan know Babe Ruth? Would a Pakistani know Larry Bird? Would a New Zealander know Jimmy Brown? Nah. But you can bet that all of them would know Pelé. In a world now brimming with celebrities identified by a single name, Pelé was among the first magnificent mononyms, owing as much to the grand traditions of Brazilian soccer as to his breathtaking skill and fame. He became a sporting missionary, a man who performed his craft in 88 countries, visited with two Popes, five emperors, 10 kings and 108 other heads of state.

When he traveled to Biafra for a match in 1968, officials promptly declared a two-day cease fire in the Nigerian civil war so that citizens on both sides of the bloody conflict could properly celebrate Pelé's presence and watch him play.

Part of Pelé's appeal arose from the pure joy he exuded while dribbling circles around his opponents. He was at different moments dubbed "Gasoline" for his energy, "Executioner" for his finishing and "Black Pearl" for the rare quality of his talent, but the chant in raucous soccer stadiums everywhere was always "Pelé! Pelé! Pelé!," a name that practically evolved into a noun meaning a unique

Pelé (opposite, center) opened the scoring in Brazil's 4–1 win over Italy in the 1970 World Cup final, his unprecedented third such title with the team.

THE RECORD

WORLD CUP

YEAR	SITE	GOALS	BRAZIL'S RESULTS
1958	Sweden	5	Defeated Sweden 5–2 in final
1962	Chile	0	Defeated Czechoslovakia 3–1 in final
1966	England	0	Lost to Hungary (3-1) and Portugal (3-1) in group play
1970	Mexico	7	Defeated Italy 4–1 in final
Total		**12**	**Three World Cup titles**

Career games played: 1363   Career goals: 1281

blend of speed, ball control and keen anticipation.

Pelé developed his unprecedented skills growing up in the Brazilian town of Baurú as part of a family so poor that he learned to play the game with his bare feet kicking a sock filled with rags or newspapers. Pelé didn't boot a real soccer ball until he was 10, yet before long he was dazzling opponents, some of them much older than he, every time he played. After signing with Santos, he led the club to championships in his first six seasons, averaging a goal per game. In 1958 came the first World Cup triumph. Before his two goals in the final, he scored three in the semifinals against France. Did we mention he was 17 at the time? It was a testament to Brazil's overall talent that they won the World Cup mostly without Pelé in '62, as he was injured in a first-round game against Czechoslovakia. In '66, when England won the Cup, Pelé was brutalized by defenders throughout the tournament, missing Brazil's second game because of injury, and his team failed to advance to the second round. But he scored a goal and assisted on two others in Brazil's 1970 championship victory over Italy to become the first and still the only man ever to play on three World Cup winners.

Pelé concluded his 22-year career in 1977 with 1,281 goals in 1,363 career matches, more than twice the scoring production of any other player living or dead. Apart from the goals he scored during his final three seasons, when he spread the soccer gospel to the U.S. as a member of the New York Cosmos, Pelé scored all of his goals for either Brazil's national team or Santos. Indeed, fearful that

Despite his enormous successes with Brazil (above, right), Pelé had lost none of his passion for the game when he arrived in the U.S. to play for the Cosmos (above, left and opposite), whom he led to the North American Soccer League title in 1977, one season after being named league MVP.

"I have had many great moments in my career, but the greatest honor was to play with Pelé."
—FRANZ BECKENBAUER, *captain of Germany's 1974 World Cup champion team and a teammate of Pelé's on the Cosmos*

"Guys were saying: 'Isn't it amazing? I can't believe it.' Pelé was in the runway, looking at the upper tier. We had expected maybe 45,000 fans, tops, and instead were getting over 60,000."
—*WERNER ROTH,*
Cosmos captain,
describing the atmosphere
before a 1977 game

he would be lured to Europe by a lucrative offer—the Italian club Juventus had promised him the then extraordinary sum of $2.5 million after the '58 World Cup—the president of Brazil, Jânio Quadros, claimed Pelé as a national treasure.

Brazil's greatest hero eventually left his country's national team in 1971 because he believed that the team's triumphs diverted attention from the evils of the nation's repressive military government. It was Edson Arantes do Nascimento who made that political decision, because Pelé could not. "Pelé doesn't have a nation, race, religion or color," he once said of himself. "People all over the world love Pelé. Edson is a man like other men. Edson is going to die someday. But Pelé doesn't die. Pelé is immortal."
                                    —*T.C.*

Spotlight

After coming out of retirement to meet one more challenge—that of spreading the "beautiful game" to America—Pelé finally called it quits in 1977 following three seasons with the New York Cosmos of the North American Soccer League. His final game was an exhibition between the Cosmos and Pelé's former club, Santos, of Brazil. (Pelé's last official game was the '77 NASL title match, in which he led the Cosmos to a 2–1 triumph over the Seattle Sounders.) Despite rainy weather, a sellout crowd of 75,646 packed Giants Stadium for the sendoff. Before the game, in which Pelé played one half for each team, he addressed the massive audience over the P.A., asking them to repeat after him: "Love … Love … Love." Through the falling rain, the thousands responded as one, repeating Pelé's refrain. He scored a goal for the Cosmos in the first half and nearly hit net for Santos in the second half, after which he was paraded around the field on the shoulders of his teammates. It is reported that Muhammad Ali, who was in Giants Stadium that day, leaned over to an acquaintance after the game and said, "Now I understand—he *is* greater than I am."

Pelé was quick, crafty and sometimes acrobatic, as he demonstrated in a 1975 NASL game (opposite), five years after he concluded his international career with a ride atop the shoulders of his admirers following Brazil's 1970 World Cup triumph in Mexico City (above).

Bill Russell

Elvin Hayes called Bill Russell the Ghost because he seemed to come out of nowhere to block shots. Red Auerbach, who coached the Boston Celtics teams Russell spearheaded, said he "put a whole new sound in the game, the sound of his footsteps. A guy would be going in all alone for a layup, and he'd hear the sound of those footsteps behind him. After this happened a few times, guys started hearing Russell's footsteps even when he wasn't there."

The idea of a man 6'9" tall with the wingspan of a Cessna being invisible is rich indeed. But players who faced the dynasty Celtics of 1956–69 played with one eye on the lookout for the leaping Russell, who seemed to own the air space in and around the lane. The Celtics won the NBA championship in 11 of his 13 seasons, and Russell was league MVP five times—remarkable accomplishments for a man with mediocre shooting skills and a workmanlike style.

Russell's greatness lay in discovering that the best defensive position was not behind the ball handler or on his hip, but in his head. A trash talker before the term was invented, Russell planted negative thoughts the way a gardener plants tulips—deeply, and with plenty of B.S. He once told the Hawks' Bill Bridges to bring salt and pepper because he was going to make Bridges eat basketballs. Russell disrupted teams by destroying their shooters' rhythm and killing their confidence.

How awkward, then, that the best statistical measure of his ability to intimidate—blocked shots—is represented in the record books by thirteen dashes. The NBA didn't keep track of blocks in Russell's time, so there isn't a numerical hint of how dominating he really was. And remember, Russell was a possession blocker. Most of his blocks were soft-handed snuffs, the ball dropping like rainwater off a leaf.

Russell didn't want bragging rights; he wanted the ball.

The fans, of course, didn't get to know Russell or get to hear his wild cackle, the most joyful in sports. His public face was one of anger and militancy. He stunned Bostonians when he said, "If Paul Revere were riding today it would be for racism: 'The niggers are coming! The niggers are coming!'" As a rookie in 1957, Russell was the Celtics' only

Russell and Wilt Chamberlain (opposite) always brought out the best in one another; theirs was one of the great rivalries in NBA history.

You can stand at a bar and scream all you want about who was the greatest athlete and which was the greatest sports dynasty, and you can shout out your precious statistics, and maybe you're right, and maybe the red-faced guy down the bar—the one with the foam on his beer and the fancy computer rankings—is right, but nobody really knows. The only thing we know for sure about superiority in sports in the United States of America in the 20th century is that Bill Russell and the Boston Celtics teams he led stand alone as the ultimate winners. Fourteen times in Russell's career it came down to one game, win you must, or lose and go home. Fourteen times the team with Bill Russell on it won....

Tommy Heinsohn, who played with Russell for nine years and won 10 NBA titles himself, as player and coach, sums it up best: "Look, all I know is, the guy won two NCAA championships, 50-some college games in a row, the ['56] Olympics, then he came to Boston and won 11 championships in 13 years, and they named a f------ tunnel after Ted Williams." By that standard, only a cathedral on a hill deserves to have Bill Russell's name attached to it.

—FRANK DEFORD
May 10, 1999

black player, and thus the only Celtic to be denied service at hotels and restaurants. He, in return, refused to sign autographs—although he sometimes flummoxed fans by offering to talk with them instead.

It would be a stretch to say that Russell, by himself, made either Boston or the NBA more hospitable to men of color. Nonetheless, he inspired such affection and respect from his teammates that the retiring Auerbach turned his position over to Russell in 1966, making the big man the first African-American head coach of a major sports franchise. In his second year as a player-coach, Russell led the Celtics to yet another title, their 10th in 12 years. They would win one more the following season. Russell's grandfather, seeing his first game of basketball in 1967, was stunned afterwards by the sight of John Havlicek, a white player, and Sam Jones, a black player, side by side in the shower. "I never thought I'd live to see the day," he told his grandson.

Whether he was snatching a rebound in front of Philadelphia's Chamberlain (above), or rejecting a shot by Elgin Baylor of the Lakers (opposite), Russell always thought defense first, and it paid off: With 11 titles in 13 years, he is arguably the greatest team player in U.S. pro sports history.

"Before Russell
came along, no one
had ever blocked
shots in the pros or
forced teams out of
their offensive
patterns. He put
a new sound in
the game, the
sound of his
footsteps."
—RED AUERBACH

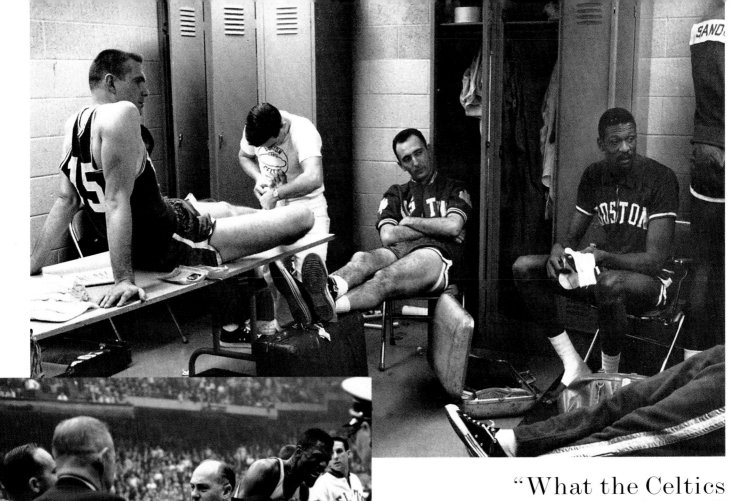

"What the Celtics
did with Russ will
never be duplicated in
a team sport. Never."
—*Bob Cousy*

THE RECORD

YEAR	TEAM	G	FG %	FT %	REB	AST	PTS	PPG	RPG
1956-57	Bos	48	.427	.492	943	88	706	14.7	19.6
1957-58	Bos	69	.442	.519	1564	202	1142	16.6	22.7
1958-59	Bos	70	.457	.598	1612	222	1168	16.7	23.0
1959-60	Bos	74	.467	.612	1778	277	1350	18.2	24.0
1960-61	Bos	78	.426	.550	1868	268	1322	16.9	23.9
1961-62	Bos	76	.457	.595	1790	341	1436	18.9	23.6
1962-63	Bos	78	.432	.555	1843	348	1309	16.8	23.6
1963-64	Bos	78	.433	.550	1930	370	1168	15.0	24.7
1964-65	Bos	78	.438	.573	1878	410	1102	14.1	24.1
1965-66	Bos	78	.415	.551	1779	371	1005	12.9	22.8
1966-67	Bos	81	.454	.610	1700	472	1075	13.3	21.0
1967-68	Bos	78	.425	.537	1451	357	977	12.5	18.6
1968-69	Bos	77	.433	.526	1484	374	762	9.9	19.3
TOTAL		**963**	**.440**	**.561**	**21,620**	**4100**	**14,522**	**15.1**	**22.5**

In the end, Russell's legacy is best measured in titles. His University of San Francisco team won back-to-back NCAA titles (1955 and '56). He led the U.S. men's team to the gold medal in the 1956 Olympics. And then came those 11 NBA rings—one for every finger, both thumbs, and an earlobe—the greatest dynasty in U.S. professional sports history. "Individual awards were mostly political," Russell wrote after his retirement, "but winning and losing, there are no politics, only numbers. It's the most democratic thing in the world."   —*J.G.*

Referee Mendy Rudolph (opposite) may not have wanted to hear what Russell had to say, but his teammates in the Celtics locker room (top) and his coach, Red Auerbach (inset, center), were always willing to listen to their fiery team leader.

Jim Thorpe

When he arrived at the 1912 Olympic Games in Stockholm, Sweden, Jim Thorpe had never before competed in a decathlon. He had never even touched a javelin until two months earlier. To the amazement of everybody except Jim Thorpe, he won the gold medal and shattered the record in the event. With a masterful performance to win the gold medal in the pentathlon, Thorpe had earned an unprecedented Olympic double. When Sweden's King Gustav V presented Thorpe with the decathlon medal the monarch proclaimed, "Sir, you are the greatest athlete in the world."

Taking the entire experience—including his own spectacular performance—in stride, Thorpe responded, "Thanks, king."

Unlike the case with modern athletes, many of Thorpe's sporting achievements cannot be measured by statistics because, for the most part, nobody kept them back then. It's a testament to Thorpe's brilliance that we don't even need them. The stories of those who witnessed Thorpe in action are enough to sustain his legend.

The great-grandson of a Sac and Fox Indian war chief, Thorpe was a college football All-America in 1911 and '12 while playing for the Carlisle (Pa.) Indian School. He quickly proved himself adept in basketball, lacrosse, swimming, wrestling, shooting and any other sport or game that he was challenged to try at Carlisle. His specialties, though, were track and football, the two sports in which he apprenticed under coach Glenn Warner, who would later become famously known as "Pop."

At a track meet against Lafayette, the 6'1", 190-pound Thorpe single-handedly secured victory for his school by winning nearly every event. On the football field, Thorpe was primarily a halfback who ran with both power and speed, but he also punted, returned kicks and passed the ball when necessary. With Thorpe, Carlisle defeated many of the powerhouse football programs of the era. In a 1912 game against Army he returned a kickoff for a touchdown only to have it called back because of a penalty. No matter. Thorpe repeated the feat on the next play. In football, as in the decathlon, Thorpe may not have been the finest at each of the individual skills he

Despite scant preparation, Thorpe (opposite) won two gold medals at the 1912 Olympics in Stockholm.

Thorpe won the pentathlon 200-meter dash (above), and hurled the javelin (opposite) respectably despite having never thrown one until two months before the Games; his world-record decathlon total would have placed second at the *1948* Olympics.

practiced, but he was far better than anybody else who aspired to do all of them—pass, run, kick or tackle—in the same game. A very reliable source from the era, legendary sportswriter Grantland Rice, wrote that Thorpe was "the greatest football player ever."

He may also have been the most natural athlete ever. He rarely indulged in the practice of practice, instead preferring a training method that has since come to be regarded as visualization. After his Olympic triumph, Thorpe played six seasons in major league baseball and parts of 13 seasons in professional football. He was enshrined in the Professional Football Hall of

Fame in 1963, in the inaugural class of 17. His story made it to Hollywood, too, in the 1951 hit film, *Jim Thorpe—All-American*, starring Burt Lancaster. In fact, Thorpe was such an enormous crowd pleaser that his public appearances did not stop with his death in 1953. In a coda that Hollywood would have left out of the script—unless Vincent Price was directing—Thorpe's wife sold his body as a tourist attraction to the highest bidder. A small village in Pennsylvania ponied up for Thorpe's remains, and also voted to change the town's name to Jim Thorpe, Pa.

Thorpe's demise was hastened by alco-

"If you're lucky, you might see real greatness
once or twice in your lifetime. You don't forget it.
And, believe me, Jim Thorpe *was* greatness."
—*ABEL KIVIAT, 1,500-meter runner on the
1912 U.S. Olympic team*

in SI's words

Jim Thorpe lived a life of high triumph and bitter despair, both of which pursue him today, almost 30 years after his death. The decision last week by the executive board of the International Olympic Committee to restore his amateur status was most gratifying to his descendants and fans. Yet it contained the futility of all posthumous gestures and thus served to remind us that the political arm twisting that led to Thorpe's reinstatement should have been done while he was still alive.

Though he never publicly pined—pining had no place in his hard-boiled nature—for the two gold medals that were taken away from him after the 1912 Olympics, members of Thorpe's family agree that his life would have been brighter without the shadow cast by the loss of the medals, on a charge of professionalism. Thorpe could have used one fewer shadow; the bottle had caused him unhappiness enough.

But even as one chapter closes on the strange and sad Thorpe saga, another remains open: that of his unrestful soul. His body lies in a small town called Jim Thorpe in northeastern Pennsylvania, which was Mauch Chunk [from a Lenni-Lenape Indian word meaning "bear mountain"] when Thorpe was alive. Thorpe presumably didn't know of the town and almost certainly he never visited it. His third wife, the late Patricia Askew Thorpe, handled the burial arrangements, and ... they were odd arrangements indeed. Thorpe's sons and daughters, meanwhile, say that his soul is doomed to wander until he is returned to his native Oklahoma and given a proper Indian burial.

—JACK McCALLUM,
October 25, 1982
[As of June 1999, Thorpe's body remains in Jim Thorpe, Pa.—Ed.]

After receiving the crushing news that his Olympic medals would be revoked, Jim Thorpe signed with the New York Giants of major league baseball in 1913. Two years later he joined the Canton Bulldogs professional football team and split his time as a pro in both sports. He retired from baseball in 1919, and his record in the sport is listed below. Statistics from Thorpe's pro football career, which lasted intermittently from 1915 to 1928, are spotty. According to NFL records, Thorpe played in 52 games for seven teams from 1920 to 1928. He threw four career touchdown passes, scored six rushing touchdowns and kicked four field goals and three extra points. The league lists no figures from Thorpe's pre-1920 career with Canton.

BASEBALL RECORD

YEAR	TEAM	G	R	HR	RBI	SB	AVG
1913	NY-N	19	6	1	2	2	.143
1914	NY-N	30	5	0	2	1	.194
1915	NY-N	17	8	0	1	4	.231
1917	Cin-N	77	29	4	36	11	.247
	NY-N	26	12	0	4	1	.193
	Yr	103	41	4	40	12	.237
1918	NY-N	58	15	1	11	3	.248
1919	NY-N	2	0	0	1	0	.333
	Bos-N	60	16	1	25	7	.327
	Yr	62	16	1	26	7	.327
TOTAL		**289**	**91**	**7**	**82**	**29**	**.252**

> "The individual laurel spray goes to Jim Thorpe, with no one close."
> — GRANTLAND RICE, sportswriter, assessing the greatest living athletes in the 1950s

holism, which was exacerbated by his lifelong grief over having to forfeit his two gold medals because he had participated in two summers of semipro baseball prior to the 1912 Olympics. Seventy years later, after tireless campaigning by his heirs, Thorpe's records and his good name were restored, and in 1983 his family received duplicates of the medals he had won at Stockholm. While Thorpe couldn't enjoy that redemption, he did live long enough to read a 1950 Associated Press poll that overwhelmingly ranked him as the best athlete of the first half of the 20th century, echoing what Sweden's King Gustav V had decreed nearly four decades earlier.

Three years after his Olympic glory (above), Thorpe donned a Canton Bulldogs uniform (opposite), and demonstrated further versatility as he kicked, passed, ran and played defense to lead Canton to unofficial pro titles in 1916, '17 and '19.

Ted Williams

When Ted Williams talked about hitting, his voice rose an octave and went up 20 decibels. He could read the seams of a baseball the way an editor reads a manuscript, and he knew pitchers better than their wives did. He mentally mapped the strike zone into grids and plotted his swing plane for maximum power and plate coverage. He practiced hitting until his blisters bled. He worked on his stance in elevators and on train platforms, using a rolled-up newspaper for a bat. "I'm as dumb as a lamppost about a lot of things," he said after his playing days. "But I think I learned a lot about hitting."

Joe DiMaggio, the Yankee Clipper, called his Red Sox rival "absolutely the best hitter I ever saw." Williams batted .406 in 1941, and no major leaguer has batted .400 since. Williams batted .344 for his 19-year career, and no modern hitter has matched that, either, not even the singles-hitting Hall of Famer, Rod Carew. To Williams, the feel of his bat soundly connecting with a pitched ball was more satisfying than a sneeze, the sound of it more fulfilling than applause. He hit 521 career home runs despite spending almost five of his prime years as a Marine pilot in two wars. "Nothing else mattered but the hitting," he said. "I lived to hit." Williams was the poster boy for monomania.

He was also a cranky bastard, but episodes at both ends of his career demonstrated why baseball fans respected and finally loved Williams. On the last day of the 1941 season, with his average at .400, the 23-year-old Boston star was invited by manager Joe Cronin to sit out a doubleheader against the A's in Philadelphia. Instead, Williams played both games and went 6 for 8, shaming all the subsequent batting champs who put their butts on the pine and not on the line. Sixteen years later, Williams homered in his last at-bat at Fenway Park, inspiring a memorable headline—HUB FANS BID KID ADIEU—and an enduring essay of the same title by John Updike.

Williams was, above all, a man's man, a Hemingway character on the hoof. On a bombing mission over Korea in 1953, Williams radioed another member of his squadron—a fairly capable pilot named John Glenn—that he was in "a little trouble." His F-9 Panther

"All I want out of life," Williams (opposite) said, "is that when I walk down the street folks will say, 'There goes the greatest hitter that ever lived.'"

Williams disdained the press (above, left), preferring the open waters of Florida (above, right) when he wasn't on the baseball diamond; as he demonstrated against the Cleveland Indians in 1955 (opposite), he had the sweetest stroke of anyone who ever played the game.

had been hit, but Williams brought the bullet-riddled plane back for a belly landing and scrambled to safety just before it was engulfed in flames. In more peaceful times, Williams could be found on his boat, a fishing rod in hand, trolling the Florida Keys one week or wading into Canada's Miramichi River the next. "I dream of bonefish, I dream of salmon," he said. "I dream of casting for them, I dream of the beautiful spots I've been."

That Williams had a temper is well documented. He shocked parsons and bluenoses when he threw bats and cussed at umpires, and he showed his contempt for newspapermen whenever he got a chance. He erupted most famously at a game against the Yankees in 1956. Booed by the Fenway fans—he had just dropped a fly ball with the bases

THE RECORD

YEAR	TEAM	G	R	HR	RBI	SB	AVG
1939	Bos-A	149	131	31	145	2	.327
1940	Bos-A	144	134	23	113	4	.344
1941	Bos-A	143	135	37	120	2	.406
1942	Bos-A	150	141	36	137	3	.356
1946	Bos-A	150	142	38	123	0	.342
1947	Bos-A	156	125	32	114	0	.343
1948	Bos-A	137	124	25	127	4	.369
1949	Bos-A	155	150	43	159	1	.343
1950	Bos-A	89	82	28	97	3	.317
1951	Bos-A	148	109	30	126	1	.318
1952	Bos-A	6	2	1	3	0	.400
1953	Bos-A	37	17	13	34	0	.407
1954	Bos-A	117	93	29	89	0	.345
1955	Bos-A	98	77	28	83	2	.356
1956	Bos-A	136	71	24	82	0	.345
1957	Bos-A	132	96	38	87	0	.388
1958	Bos-A	129	81	26	85	1	.328
1959	Bos-A	103	32	10	43	0	.254
1960	Bos-A	113	56	29	72	1	.316
TOTAL		**2292**	**1798**	**521**	**1839**	**24**	**.344**

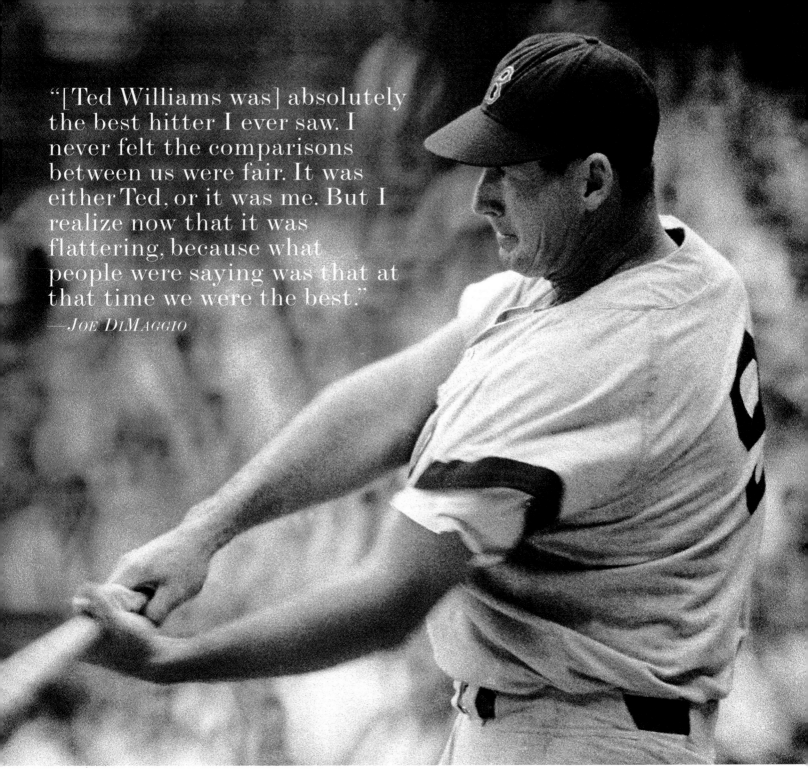

"[Ted Williams was] absolutely the best hitter I ever saw. I never felt the comparisons between us were fair. It was either Ted, or it was me. But I realize now that it was flattering, because what people were saying was that at that time we were the best."
—JOE DIMAGGIO

Spotlight

Certainly the best hitter of his generation, and very possibly the best of all time, Ted Williams, a.k.a. the Splendid Splinter, the Kid and Thumper, had 2,654 career hits from which to choose his favorite. He could have picked the final at-bat of his career, in 1960, when he capped his 19 seasons in the majors with a flourish by hitting a home run. Or he could have chosen his first at-bat in 1946, when, returning to the majors after spending three years in the Marines, the Kid belted a home run on the very first pitch thrown to him. He could have selected the time later that season when he stroked an inside-the-park home run the opposite way against a defense employing the fabled "Williams shift." But the clout Williams calls his "most thrilling hit" comes from the 1941 All-Star Game in Detroit. The American League team trailed 5–4 in the bottom of the ninth with two outs and two men on base, one of whom was Joe DiMaggio, who was in the midst of his legendary 56-game hitting streak. Williams stepped to the plate against Claude Passeau of the Chicago Cubs and pasted a three-run homer to the upper deck in right field to give the AL a 7–5 victory. The Yankee Clipper was waiting to congratulate him at home plate.

"He had a very
curious mind,
always studying
the pitcher,
always picking
someone's brain."
—*CURT GOWDY*,
*broadcaster,
on Williams*

loaded—Williams spit at the left field stands, spit at the right field stands, and then stepped back out of the dugout and spit again, like a tenor answering calls for an encore. "He always wanted to be perfect," said one of his pals, a Florida fishing guide. "And when he wasn't, he'd get mad."

Just as often, Williams showed a generous side, and the fan who dared approach him on the street was likely to be rewarded with a sparkling discourse on baseball or life. But the Williams legacy will always be his swing, that glorious blend of stride and torque that resulted in his ineffably gorgeous follow-through. "Hitting a baseball," he said, "is the single most difficult thing to do in sport."

Ted Williams put the lie to his own claim by making it look so easy.   —J.G.

No one was better prepared or more focused in the on-deck circle (opposite) or at the plate (top) than Williams, who, not coincidentally, received more than his share of intentional walks; off the field (above), hitting was Williams's favorite topic of conversation.

Greatness
Visible

Greatness Visible

After completing this final chapter the knowledgeable reader might well wonder, *Where have you gone, Joe DiMaggio?* It's an excellent question.

Among the athletes who don't appear in our closing section are a list of sporting luminaries totally unaccustomed to missing the cut in anything. For every athlete we chose there was inevitably somebody else in his or her sport, sometimes even on his or her team, who had a legitimate argument to join the club. For instance, DiMaggio and his extraordinary 56-game hitting streak were nosed out by his Yankees successor, Mickey Mantle, and such significant baseball pioneers as Ty Cobb, Lou Gehrig and Jackie Robinson were also left out.

Among great basketball players, while Larry Bird and Magic Johnson, forever linked by their stirring rivalry, both made our list, Johnson's teammate Kareem Abdul-Jabbar was among the final omissions. This despite Abdul-Jabbar's having finished his career as the leading scorer in NBA history. Oscar Robertson, too, hit the cutting room floor, despite being the only player ever to average a triple-double in a season. Joe Montana gets his due, but where would he have been without his partner, Jerry Rice, who was excluded from our final 25 despite catching more passes than any other receiver in NFL history? And looking back further in pro football history, Red Grange and Don Hutson got the nod while brilliant quarterbacks Sammy Baugh and Otto Graham, and the versatile Ernie Nevers, who also played pro baseball, fell short.

We chose Martina Navratilova but not her brilliant antagonists, Chris Evert and Steffi Graf, or her outstanding predecessor, Margaret Smith Court. We also excluded Billie Jean King, who laid the groundwork for modern women's tennis in several ways, most notably by beating Bobby Riggs in the celebrated Battle of the Sexes in 1973. On the men's side, while Rod Laver grand slammed his way into the mix, we labored over the exclusion of more modern tennis monarchs like Pete Sampras and John McEnroe. We selected Jack Nicklaus at the expense of Arnold Palmer, who won 60 PGA tournaments, including seven majors, and made golf a fashionable sport for his heir apparent to rule.

Jackie Joyner-Kersee cleared the bar, while such legendary Olympic athletes as Wilma Rudolph, Paavo Nurmi, Jesse Owens and even Edwin Moses did not. Wayne Gretzky would be the first to insist that he should have been joined in this book by his idol, Gordie Howe, whose many scoring records Gretzky shattered. Joe Louis knocked off our list the likes of Jack Dempsey and Sugar Ray Robinson, great champions in their own right.

We salute all the legendary athletes who do not appear in the following pages, and emphasize that where this list is concerned, there is no shame in finishing 26th.

—*T.C.*

Our list was the only cut the great Robertson (above) or the legendary DiMaggio (opposite) failed to make in their superlative careers.

Hank Aaron

Different men handled segregation in different ways. Jackie Robinson, who broke the color line in major league baseball, confronted it. Buck O'Neil, the Negro League baseball star, deflected it with good humor. But Henry Aaron, a child of the Jim Crow South and a star slugger for the Braves, had his own way of handling racial insults. He collected them. Counted them. Put them under the microscope and studied their genes. Twenty years after "Dear Nigger" letters jammed his mailbox while he was chasing Babe Ruth's hallowed career home run record, Aaron would get out the worst ones and re-read them. "I read the letters," he said, "because they remind me not to be surprised or hurt. They remind me of what people are really like."

Like many collectors, Aaron was a quiet man, his pessimism about human nature hidden behind a calm professionalism. He was a lifetime .305 hitter with a wristy, whiplike stroke. He led the National League in home runs and RBIs four times each and played in 21 All-Star Games. He set career records for runs, total bases, extra-base hits and, of course, home runs. He eventually caught and ran past Ruth's total of 714 dingers (Aaron finished with 755), but he never ran out from under his hat like Willie Mays. Nor did he glower from the mound like Bob Gibson. "You couldn't read him," said one of Aaron's teammates, "because he wouldn't let anything show."

The Magnavox Corporation, makers of television sets, signed Aaron to a five-year, million-dollar promotional contract in 1974, as he closed in on Ruth's record. But Magnavox stopped using Aaron after two and a half years; as a pitchman, he was too shy and reserved. When a poll of writers, broadcasters and baseball executives failed to select him as player of the decade for the 1970s, an angry Aaron finally erupted. "You have a Chicago writer who was born with a silver spoon in his mouth," he said. "He don't know how Henry Aaron feels, 'cause he's never walked in my shoes. He's never been a black man in his life, he ain't never been told he couldn't eat in a restaurant."

What happened during Aaron's pursuit of Ruth's record disillusioned people who pictured America as a harmonious melting pot. In 1973,

Hammerin' Hank (opposite) pounded out yet another excellent season in 1964, when he hit 24 homers, drove in 95 runs and batted .328.

THE RECORD

YEAR	TEAM	G	R	HR	RBI	SB	AVG
1954	Mil-N	122	58	13	69	2	.280
1955	Mil-N	153	105	27	106	3	.314
1956	Mil-N	153	106	26	92	2	.328
1957	Mil-N	151	118	44	132	1	.322
1958	Mil-N	153	109	30	95	4	.326
1959	Mil-N	154	116	39	123	8	.355
1960	Mil-N	153	102	40	126	16	.292
1961	Mil-N	155	115	34	120	21	.327
1962	Mil-N	156	127	45	128	15	.323
1963	Mil-N	161	121	44	130	31	.319
1964	Mil-N	145	103	24	95	22	.328
1965	Mil-N	150	109	32	89	24	.318
1966	Atl-N	158	117	44	127	21	.279
1967	Atl-N	155	113	39	109	17	.307
1968	Atl-N	160	84	29	86	28	.287
1969	Atl-N	147	100	44	97	9	.300
1970	Atl-N	150	103	38	118	9	.298
1971	Atl-N	139	95	47	118	1	.327
1972	Atl-N	129	75	34	77	4	.265
1973	Atl-N	120	84	40	96	1	.301
1974	Atl-N	112	47	20	69	1	.268
1975	Mil-A	137	45	12	60	0	.234
1976	Mil-A	85	22	10	35	0	.229
TOTAL		**3298**	**2174**	**755**	**2297**	**240**	**.305**

as his career homer total surpassed 700, Aaron received more than 3,000 letters a day. Many were hateful; a few threatened to kill him or kidnap his children. The letters proved that all too many Americans rejected the civil rights movement of the '60s and the notion of equality for all.

But the letters did not tell the whole story. When 40,000 Atlanta fans gave Aaron a five-minute standing ovation after his last at-bat of the 1973 season—he had popped out to second, one homer short of Ruth—Aaron was as confused as he was overwhelmed. "I took off my cap and held it up in the air," he said later, "and then I turned in a circle and looked at all those people standing and clapping ... and to tell you the truth, I didn't know how to feel. I don't think I'd ever felt so good in my life. But I wasn't ready for it."

He was the last Negro Leaguer to play in the

A marvel of versatility as well as consistency, Aaron had good speed on the basepaths (above) and always stirred fear in the hearts of opposing pitchers when he took his place in the on-deck circle (opposite).

"Hank made everything look easy. Mays did everything with flair, but he never made the perfect throws to the cutoff man the way Hank did. Hank was just so smooth about everything. He was the best all-around player I ever saw."

—*LEW BURDETTE,*
Braves pitcher

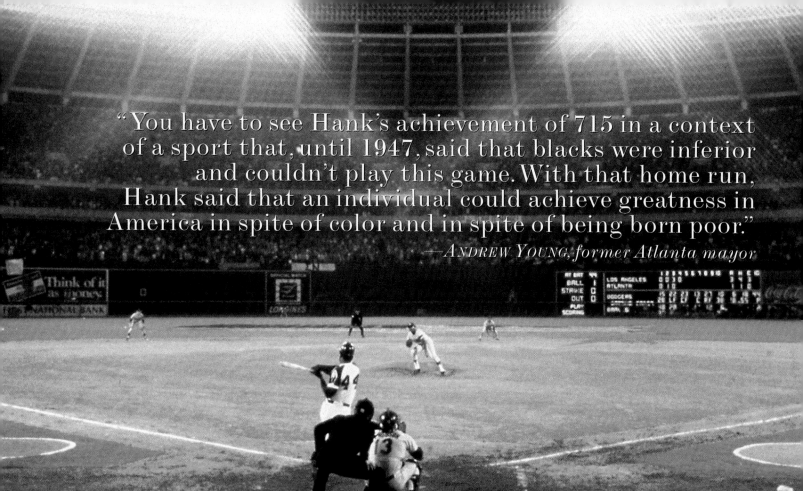

"You have to see Hank's achievement of 715 in a context of a sport that, until 1947, said that blacks were inferior and couldn't play this game. With that home run, Hank said that an individual could achieve greatness in America in spite of color and in spite of being born poor."
—ANDREW YOUNG, *former Atlanta mayor*

majors. As a shortstop for the Indianapolis Clowns of the Negro League in 1952, and later as a kid outfielder in the historically white Sally League, Aaron had focused on the barriers he knew he could overcome—ballpark fences. But his experiences made him blind to the barriers that fell around him in the '60s. When he finally passed Ruth, on April 8, 1974, skyrockets exploded in the Atlanta sky and 53,775 fans cheered their heads off. Yet Aaron was still nagged by the threats, the insensitive newspaper columns. "It should have been the most enjoyable time in my life," he said. "And instead it was hell."

That sentiment is as crushing as Aaron's record-breaking blast to the left field bullpen off the Dodgers' Al Downing on that April night. —J.G.

Aaron wore uniform No. 44 (inset) for all of his 23 seasons, though he donned No. 55 for a spring training game in 1957 (opposite); Aaron's brilliant career reached a memorable climax when he belted his 715th career home run (top) to eclipse Babe Ruth's record.

Update

In 1999 Major League Baseball embarked on a season-long commemoration of the 25th anniversary of Hank Aaron's career home run record. The recognition was somewhat overdue. When Aaron hit career home run No. 715 to eclipse Babe Ruth's legendary record on April 8, 1974, baseball commissioner Bowie Kuhn didn't even attend the game. But the 1999 celebration, which began on April 8 with Aaron's being honored by a sellout crowd at Atlanta's new Turner Field (Atlanta-Fulton County Stadium, where Aaron hit the famous clout, has been razed), seeks to put things right.

Aaron, who is now a senior vice president with the Braves and a Turner Broadcasting executive, will appear in 20 major league stadiums during the summer of '99 and will star in television and print advertisements promoting the celebration. He has also collaborated on a book with sportswriter Dick Schaap, *Home Run: My Life in Pictures*. It represents a rare moment of self-concern for Aaron, who has spent his post-baseball career helping others. He created the Chasing the Dream Foundation, which offers grants to youngsters to help them achieve their goals in art, sports and music. He serves on the executive board of, among other institutions, the NAACP and Morehouse College, and he has forcefully prodded major league baseball to improve its poor record of minority hirings. Aaron was also the Braves' director of player development for 13 years. During that time he acquired for Atlanta players such as David Justice and Tom Glavine—proof that he had not lost touch with the game. In 1999 the game will be getting back in touch with Aaron.

Larry Bird

Larry Bird never really left French Lick, Indiana, the little sulfur-spring resort where his waitress mother raised four normal sons, a normal daughter, and Larry—a chimera.

Four years at Indiana State didn't change him much, and neither did 13 seasons as an NBA superstar. A Boston Celtics teammate visited Bird's home once and was amazed when breakfast was interrupted by a bunch of Larry's pals, just back from a hunting trip in a truck "full of dead deer and empty bottles of Jack Daniel's." There was always about Bird the whiff of small-town garage, the echo of barber shop conversation. His alcoholic father committed suicide. His grandma took him in to relieve the crush at home. "I don't like crowds, never have," said the man who attracted them to NBA arenas. "And the unexpected has always bothered me."

They called him "the hick from French Lick," and when he joined the Celtics he was certainly unpolished, a gawky giant with unruly, straw-colored hair. In college, Bird had refused to be interviewed for most of

Bird (left) was not a great leaper, nor was he particularly graceful, yet he averaged 10 rebounds and 24.3 points per game during his 13-year NBA career.

"He has an instinct, a natural feeling for the sport, vision, long arms, unselfish attitude and everything else you might want to order."
—BOB COUSY

THE RECORD

YEAR	TEAM	G	FG%	FT%	REB	AST	PTS	PPG	RPG
1979-80	Bos	82	.474	.836	852	370	1745	21.3	10.4
1980-81	Bos	82	.478	.863	895	451	1741	21.2	10.9
1981-82	Bos	77	.503	.863	837	447	1761	22.9	10.9
1982-83	Bos	79	.504	.840	870	458	1867	23.6	11.0
1983-84	Bos	79	.492	.888	796	520	1908	24.2	10.1
1984-85	Bos	80	.522	.882	842	531	2295	28.7	10.2
1985-86	Bos	82	.496	.896	805	557	2115	25.8	9.8
1986-87	Bos	74	.525	.910	682	566	2076	28.1	9.2
1987-88	Bos	76	.527	.916	703	467	2275	29.9	9.3
1988-89	Bos	6	.471	.947	37	29	116	19.3	6.2
1989-90	Bos	75	.473	.930	712	562	1820	24.3	9.5
1990-91	Bos	60	.454	.891	509	431	1164	19.4	8.5
1991-92	Bos	45	.466	.927	434	306	908	20.2	9.6
TOTAL		**897**	**.496**	**.886**	**8974**	**5695**	**21,791**	**24.3**	**10.0**

1979, claiming he had been misquoted early in the season and that his Indiana State teammates were as responsible for the Sycamores' run to the '79 NCAA finals as he was. This was not true—ISU, with four starters returning, went 16–11 the season after Bird departed—but Larry didn't care. He remembered that nobody had been interested in him in 1974, when, after 24 days as an Indiana University freshman and a spell in junior college, he had dropped out and taken a job feeding the maw of a French Lick garbage truck.

Bird was reticent, so you had to read his game to glimpse the inner man. His deadly shooting from the foul line and from 3-point range spoke of self-discipline. His unorthodox, from-the-right-ear delivery showed a gift for invention—or maybe stubbornness. Bird's rebounding was predatory and calculating; he

Bird was a complete player who could drive to the hoop, as he did during his rookie season of 1979–80, soaring over another legend, Pete Maravich of the Utah Jazz (opposite), or fearlessly dive for a loose ball, as he did in 1989 against the Lakers (above).

knew all the angles and all the gritty tricks of blocking out. His passing? As natural as a reflex, as personal as a signature. "Look in his eyes," said Atlanta's Dominique Wilkins, "and you see a killer." Watch him play, said the legendary Celtics guard Bob Cousy, and you saw "the best player who ever played this foolish game."

It is impossible to praise Bird, of course, without extolling the virtues of his longtime rival, Earvin (Magic) Johnson. The two met for the first time in that NCAA final in March 1979, when Johnson's Michigan State team beat Bird's previously undefeated Sycamores, 75–64. They then entered the NBA together—Bird as rookie of the year, Johnson

as catalyst of the league-champion Los Angeles Lakers—and wound up reviving the moribund league. Their teams met 19 times in postseason play, and when the clock was winding down you knew that either Bird or Johnson would have the ball. It was black vs. white, Showtime vs. Shytime. But Bird and Magic had more in common than met the eye. Both were big men with point-guard skills. Both were brilliant passers. Both were so dedicated to the team concept that *Sports Illustrated*'s Jack McCallum credited them with "bringing the art of unselfishness back to the game."

For his career, Bird averaged about 6 assists, 10 rebounds and 24 points a game, but as

Bird (above) wore No. 33 in college at Indiana State, which he led to an undefeated regular season and the NCAA championship game in 1979, and in the pros, where he closed his legendary career with three titles, three MVP awards and an emotional farewell at Boston Garden (opposite).

Celtics general manager Red Auerbach once said, "The one thing you have to avoid when you talk about Bird is statistics." Similarly, you couldn't judge Bird by his physique (shapeless), his leaping ability (nil) or his style (roughhouse). He threw up some of the ugliest wrong-handed shots this side of an elementary school game—"I'm like a gymnast," he once joked, "I'm into degree of difficulty"—but he almost always made the shots when it counted.

Larry Bird was more than the sum of his basketball parts. He was a small town anomaly. He was an Edgar Lee Masters poem come to life. He was a doomed kid who, given a thousand lifetimes, would have ended up drinking beer in his undershirt in 999 of them.

It was the NBA's good fortune that Bird beat those thousand-to-one odds.　　—*J.G.*

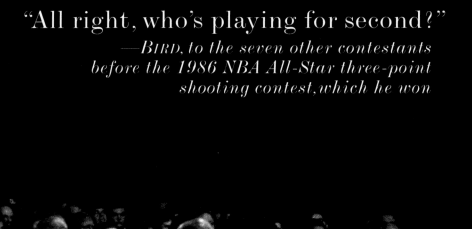

LARRY... THANK YOU FOR 13 GREAT SEASONS

"All right, who's playing for second?"
——*BIRD, to the seven other contestants before the 1986 NBA All-Star three-point shooting contest, which he won*

Update

During their six-title run in the 1990s the Chicago Bulls of Michael Jordan and Scottie Pippen were taken to a seventh game of a play-off series on only two occasions. The first was in the 1992 Eastern Conference semifinals against the Knicks, and the second came in the 1998 Eastern Conference finals against the Indiana Pacers. Those Pacers included fine players such as

deadeye shooter Reggie Miller and big man Rik Smits, but their greatest asset never even took the court. That was Larry Bird. Coach Larry Bird.

In his first season in charge of the Pacers, the man they called Larry Legend as a player—he retired in 1992—proved he could handle himself just fine, thank you, as a coach. Naysayers had claimed

that Bird would fizzle out—much as Magic Johnson had in a coaching stint with the Lakers before him—in disgust with the modern player's work ethic and will to win, which couldn't possibly compare to what his had been. Bird proved them wrong. The Indiana native led the Pacers to a 58–24 record and won plaudits for the very thing skeptics had questioned: his ability to handle

players. They respected his status as a former NBA superstar and consummate winner, and he instilled confidence in young players such as guard Jalen Rose, while reviving it in veterans like point guard Mark Jackson. The Pacers lost to the Bulls 88–83 in that tense Game 7, but Bird would be named 1997–98 NBA Coach of the Year—and he was just getting started.

Jim Brown

"I've always had my freedom," Jim Brown once said. "The price I paid for it was popularity and money." It was a revealing remark. Of all the 20th century's great athletes, Brown was the one who most consistently saw himself outside the frame of sports stardom. He carried the ball for the Cleveland Browns for only nine seasons—leading the NFL in rushing in eight of them—and when he left the game it was because he wanted to, because there were other things he wanted to accomplish. Brown starred in Hollywood action flicks and broke racial taboos—he did a love scene with Raquel Welch in *100 Rifles*—but he also steered himself into black activism, founding and leading the Black Economic Union and later working with gang leaders and convicts for a program aptly named Amer-I-Can.

"I deal with reality," Brown said.

Defiance was his touchstone. On the screen Brown expressed it with a bouncer's scowl. In the flesh he communicated it with an exaggerated bluntness, demolishing cultural and political totems. But he was not a snarling brute. At Syracuse University, where he lettered in basketball and was an All-America in football and lacrosse, Brown maintained a B average. Later, in debates with "the man"—'60s lingo for the white establishment—he maintained a tone of reason. "The most unexpected thing about Jim Brown is his speaking voice," wrote a *New York Times* movie reporter. "Even when he is saying inflammatory things, the voice remains gentle."

Brown's gifts as a running back surpassed those of anybody who had ever played the position and possibly everybody who has played it since. He was strong, fast, graceful and capable of rabbit-like acceleration. Most of all, he was durable. To stop Jim Brown, teams gang-tackled, leg-whipped, speared, punched and eye-gouged him; but after every play he got up slowly and walked back to the huddle, seemingly immune to pain. He played an entire season with a fractured big toe. He once played the second half of a game against the Giants with one eye closed, after someone ground sand from the baseball infield into it. "He took more punishment than any man in the history of this game," said Art Modell, then owner of the Browns. But the great fullback played in 118 straight games from 1957 until his retire-

Brown (opposite) earned his rest during the 1963 season, in which he averaged 6.4 yards per carry and gained 1,863 yards rushing in 14 games.

THE RECORD

YEAR	TEAM	G	ATT	RUSH. YDS	AVG	TD
1957	Cle	12	202	942	4.7	9
1958	Cle	12	257	1527	5.9	17
1959	Cle	12	290	1329	4.6	14
1960	Cle	12	215	1257	5.8	9
1961	Cle	14	305	1408	4.6	8
1962	Cle	14	230	996	4.3	13
1963	Cle	14	291	1863	6.4	12
1964	Cle	14	280	1446	5.2	7
1965	Cle	14	289	1544	5.3	17
TOTAL		**118**	**2359**	**12312**	**5.2**	**106**

ment after the 1965 season, scored 126 touchdowns and had 58 100-yard games.

Brown's numbers should probably be multiplied by a factor of, say, 1.7, because yards came tougher in his day. The NFL's hash marks were closer to the sidelines then, limiting running room on the side of the field the ball was on. Brown's short gains typically saw him dragging three or four defenders for a yard or two before he was pushed back by the pack and slammed to the ground. His big gainers were usually dances through downtown traffic in which he absorbed hits, spun off tackles, veered unpredictably and stiff-armed defenders into the turf—and then outran the secondary. On one memorable touchdown run in the Cotton Bowl—a three-yarder—Brown took hits from Dallas Cowboys legends Bob Lilly and Lee Roy Jordan, retreated ten yards, and then fought through practically everybody else in a Cowboys uniform before spinning and churning into the end zone. On another occasion Brown

> "I don't ever recall Jim Brown taking himself out of a game or a play, whether to recover from a bump or a bruise to the head. I do not recall him ever even missing a down in the five years that he played for me."
> —ART MODELL, *former owner of the Cleveland Browns*

Update

Jim Brown never made the football comeback he talked about in 1983, deciding instead to concentrate on comebacks of a different sort. In 1988 he founded a program called Amer-I-Can, whose goal is to help inmates, ex-convicts and gang members make a positive change in their lives. With a five-week, 15-step program that uses a curriculum designed by Brown, Amer-I-Can aims to improve the life skills of troubled youths in such areas as job skills, family responsibility, conflict resolution and finance management. "You must take responsibility for yourself," says Brown, whose father virtually vanished from his life when Brown was two weeks old. "The first lesson I teach in Amer-I-Can is that no one is cursed from birth. Success is for those who want it and take action to get it."

So far, the program has a presence in 14 states, and Brown is lobbying to expand it. More than 4,000 inmates in New Jersey and over 17,000 in California have participated in Amer-I-Can, which the late Tom Bradley, a former mayor of Los Angeles, called "the kernel of a major, major breakthrough." Brown also employs former gang members as advisers to police departments on their dealings with street gangs.

Despite his intense involvement in Amer-I-Can, Brown has not let his film career languish. In 1996 he appeared in the anti-gang film *Original Gangstas*, as well as in the Tim Burton spoof, *Mars Attacks!*.

Brown departed Yankee Stadium (opposite) with an escort—something he scarcely needed on the field—after the Browns beat the New York Giants in 1964, by which time Cleveland coach Paul Brown (above, middle), had departed the club and been replaced by Blanton Collier.

crashed into Giants linebacker Sam Huff so hard that Huff's helmet smashed into his nose and broke it, along with two teeth. Said Huff, "I woke up on the trainer's table."

In hindsight, the most impressive thing about Brown is that he quit when he was on top. He retired at 30, bowing out after an MVP season in which he averaged 5.3 yards per carry. Had he kept playing, he might have set unbreakable yardage and touchdown records. The thought must have occurred to him, because in 1983, when he was 47, Brown contemplated a comeback with the Los Angeles Raiders. "The standards today are lower … and the expectations are less," he said. "I can't accept quarterbacks sliding and running backs running out of bounds."

The price Brown ultimately paid for his freedom was seeing lesser talents erase his records.
—J.G.

Defenses dreaded to see Brown, who led the league in rushing for eight of his nine seasons, take a handoff (top) and rumble downfield behind the sizable frame of guard John Wooten (No. 60, right, and above).

"Look at Jim Brown. What a man. If we all could do what he does, we'd have a pretty great country."
—RON WOLFLEY, *former Cleveland Browns running back*

Red Grange

Was Red Grange ever tackled? If he was, you'd have a hard time finding proof. Grange is a football tintype whose exploits most folks of his era came to know through heroic weekly newsreel footage at the movie theater on Main Street. Those raw film clips flickering by at 18 frames a second somehow served to embellish the myth of Grange's elusiveness, perhaps because it seemed as though every time he touched the ball he dashed to the end zone. Three yards and a cloud of dust this was not. With apologies to Dominique Wilkins, Red Grange was the original human highlight film.

Those of us who never witnessed Grange for ourselves are left to rely on the eyes of the times, like those peering from the mug of legendary writer Damon Runyon. He once described Grange as "three or four men and a horse rolled into one. He is Jack Dempsey, Babe Ruth, Al Jolson, Paavo Nurmi and Man o' War."

But Harold "Red" Grange was no celebrity chimera, and—appearances on the football field to the contrary—he did not have any equine blood coursing through his veins. Grange was born in Forksville, Pa., and raised in Wheaton, Ill., where his father was chief of police. As a boy Grange never wavered in his belief that his dad was the toughest customer he ever met. Football was practically an afterthought for him; he went out for the team in high school only because the fancy uniform came free. It turned out to be the right decision for the kid they called Red because of the mop of auburn hair hidden beneath his leather helmet. He would go on to score 75 touchdowns in his three varsity seasons and would also excel in basketball and track. During the summer, the young Grange built his strength and endurance for those sports by delivering massive blocks of ice that he carried on his shoulders.

The Grange legend grew casually. He attended the University of Illinois not because of a cushy scholarship offer but because it was the cheapest college available. Before his varsity debut as a sophomore in 1923, he donned the now famous No. 77 sweater not as a plot to make him doubly lucky but because the guy before him in line was issued No. 76 and the guy behind him

Grange was not only a breathtaking runner, but also a fine defensive back and a solid placekicker, both at Illinois (right) and in the NFL.

The first game matched the Bears against the Chicago [now Phoenix] Cardinals. Accustomed to attracting crowds of less than 5,000, [Chicago Bears owner, coach and starting right end George] Halas was not prepared for the demand. The 20,000 tickets he had printed were sold in three hours. More had to be ordered. A standing room–only crowd of 36,000 jammed into Cubs Park (now known as Wrigley Field) on a snowy day. No NFL game had drawn near that number. Halas was said to have cried while counting the receipts.

St. Louis, Washington, Boston, Pittsburgh ... the trains carrying the Galloping Ghost and his supporting cast of 17 mortal Bears rumbled across the East and Midwest, and wherever they went it was the same. Grange was an event, a happening so stupendous that the curiosity to see him seemed insatiable. The Bears played before an NFL-record 40,000 fans in Philadelphia in a steady downpour, and Grange scored the game's only two touchdowns. The next day, wearing the same muddy jerseys, the Bears were cheered by 73,000 fans at the Polo Grounds in New York as Chicago beat the Giants 19–7. The $130,000 take saved [Giants owner Tim] Mara from financial ruin. "My worries," he said, "are over."

... In Detroit, nursing a torn muscle and a blood clot in his left arm, and bone tired from the killing pace ("Deep lines showed about Red's face," wrote Ford Frick) Grange could not play. More than 20,000 fans demanded refunds. That game and the next one the following day in Chicago were his only no-shows. "In those days," Grange said later, "you were taken off the field only if you could not walk or breathe."
—JOHN UNDERWOOD
Sept. 4, 1985

No. 78. Before long, though, Grange's exploits at Illinois earned him a second nickname, the Galloping Ghost. His most famous performance came on Oct. 18, 1924, in Champaign, when the Illini faced a Michigan team that hadn't lost in 20 games. Grange took the opening kickoff 95 yards for a touchdown. Minutes later he broke through the Wolverines defensive line and dashed 67 yards for another score. The next two times Illinois got the ball Grange juked and straight-armed his way for touchdowns of 56 and 45 yards. The first quarter had not yet ended, and Grange had been in the Michigan end zone four times. As he walked to the bench he received a five-minute standing ovation from the 67,000 delirious fans. And there was more to come. Grange added a fifth rushing touchdown and passed for one more in the 39–14 Illinois victory.

Grange played only 20 games in his Illinois career, but he made the most of them, scoring 31 touchdowns and rushing for 3,637 yards. The day after his final college game, the greatest open-field runner ever to play the game made a move that many observers considered his most astonishing. He signed a pro football contract, single-handedly legitimizing the fledgling professional league, which theretofore had been considered a ragtag,

"A waitress dropped a bowl of Roquefort dressing on my new blue suit in Chicago one night. I hopped up and was dancing around all excited, and there sat Red, looking at me ever so sweet-ly. 'I thought you ordered Thousand Island,' he said."

—*LINDSEY NELSON, sports broadcaster*

Billed as "the nation's idol," Grange appeared in the film *One Minute to Play* (opposite) in 1926, and while his celebrity led to publicity photos (above) harkening back to Grange's summer job as an ice hauler, it did not prevent him from receiving a speeding ticket in Tampa, Fla. (top).

"[Grange's signing was an event] comparable to the national televising of games."
—GEORGE HALAS, *Chicago Bears owner, discussing Grange's impact on the viability of pro football*

lowly outfit. Grange embarked on a whirlwind national tour with George Halas's Chicago Bears. The schedule initially called for 10 games in 17 days but was eventually expanded to 19 games in 66 days as Grange drew standing-room only crowds from St. Louis to Boston. Before Grange arrived, newspaper accounts of pro football games were buried in the back pages. The Ghost's barnstorming tour with the Bears commanded front-page headlines. The Bears-Giants game at the Polo Grounds on Dec. 6, 1925, drew an unprecedented 73,000 fans.

Grange would play nine pro seasons before retiring in 1934, a year in which he once broke into the clear and appeared headed for a touchdown, only to be caught from behind by a lineman; age and a knee injury had slowed the Galloping Ghost to a canter. Somebody did the math and found that in 237 football games, Grange carried the ball 4,013 times for 32,820 yards—an average of 8.1 yards per carry—and scored 531 touchdowns. The only mind not boggled by those numbers was that of Grange himself. "If you have the football and 11 guys are after you, if you're smart, you'll run," Grange once said. "It was no big deal."

Fortunately, there were plenty of poet-journalists in the Golden Age of American sports, and it was left to the finest of them all, Grantland Rice, to capture the elusive Grange:

> *There are two shapes now moving,*
> *Two ghosts that drift and glide,*
> *And which of them to tackle*
> *Each rival must decide;*
> *They shift with spectral swiftness*
> *Across the swarded range,*
> *And one of them's a shadow,*
> *And one of them is Grange.*

—T.C.

YEAR	TEAM	G	ATT	RUSH. YARDS	AVG	TD
1925	Chi-B	5	—	—	—	3
1927	NYY	13	—	—	—	1
1929	Chi-B	14	—	—	—	2
1930	Chi-B	14	—	—	—	8
1931	Chi-B	13	—	—	—	7
1932	Chi-B	12	57	136	2.4	7
1933	Chi-B	13	81	277	3.4	1
1934	Chi-B	12	32	156	4.9	3
TOTAL		**96**	**170**	**569**	**3.3**	**32**

Note: Rushing statistics from 1925–31 not available.

A far cry from his college days at Illinois (above, right), Grange's barnstorming tour, which SI called "the 66 days that made pro football," drew 73,000 fans to the Polo Grounds, where Grange (opposite, with ball) led the Bears to a 19–7 win over the Giants.

Don Hutson

"The thing you remember best about him was how calm and relaxed he always was," coaching great Bear Bryant said about receiver Don Hutson, his college teammate.

"He could go to sleep on the bench before the Rose Bowl game."

But once the game began, Hutson was the antithesis of Rip Van Winkle. He was, you might say, the man who woke up football.

The most money Hutson ever earned in a year as a football player was $15,000, in 1945—putting the Arkansas native in that sad category of inventors who failed to profit from their genius. When he was an end at the University of Alabama in the 1930s, Hutson collaborated with quarterback Dixie Howell to expand the idea that gave American football its zest and spectator appeal—the forward pass. Later, when he played professionally for the Green Bay Packers, Hutson choreographed the whole panoply of pass routes, buttonhooks, quits and Z-outs over which coaches have subsequently broken chalk. "I don't think there's any doubt that Don Hutson was the greatest receiver ever," Washington Redskins coach George Allen wrote in 1982. "He improvised moves and devised patterns that have been copied ever since."

Hutson's patterns were easier to copy than his moves. In an age when pro football resembled a brawl between slow-footed street gangs, Hutson had 9.7 speed in the 100-yard dash, more tricks than a magician and butter-soft hands. He was the Alabama Antelope, darting between defenders and catching passes no one else could catch. "He would glide downfield," Packers coach Curly Lambeau once said, "leaning forward as if to steady himself close to the ground. Then, as suddenly as you gulp or blink an eye, he would feint one way and go the other, reach up like a dancer, gracefully squeeze the ball and leave the scene of the accident—the accident being the defensive backs who tangled their feet up and fell trying to cover him."

In a game against the Cleveland Rams, Hutson beat the speedy Dante Magnani on a crossing pattern by hooking his left arm on the right goalpost and spinning around the upright, his feet off the ground, for a one-handed touchdown catch. ("Wasn't a bad

Hutson (right) caught bushels of passes in his 11-year career, including 99 touchdown receptions, an NFL record that stood for 44 years.

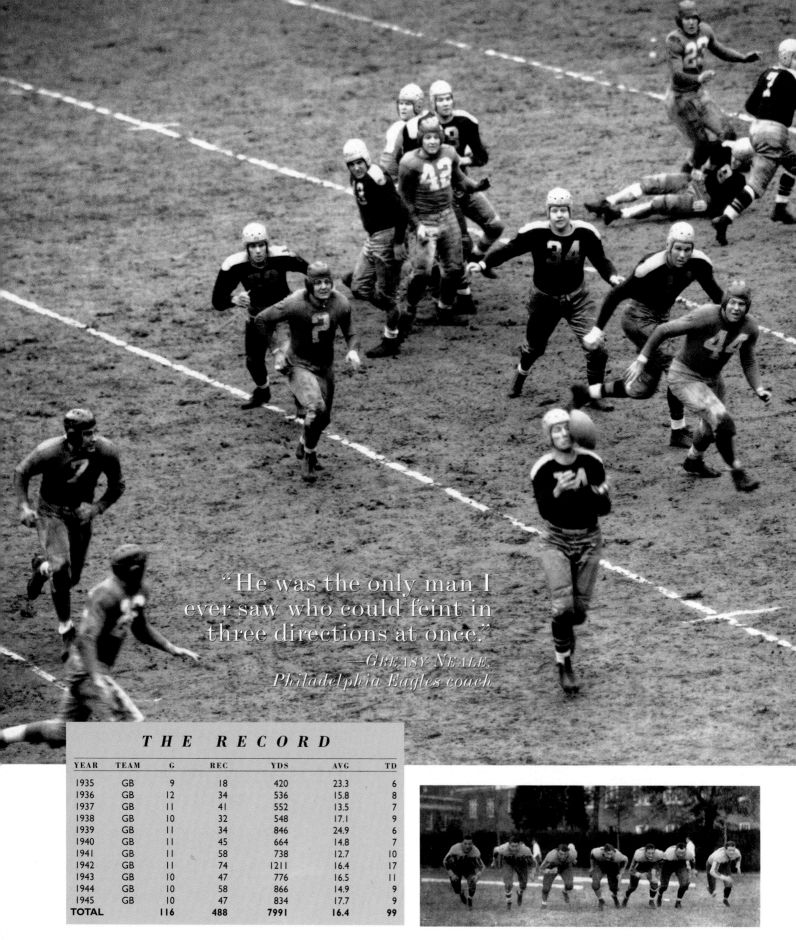

"He was the only man I ever saw who could feint in three directions at once."

—GREASY NEALE,
Philadelphia Eagles coach

THE RECORD

YEAR	TEAM	G	REC	YDS	AVG	TD
1935	GB	9	18	420	23.3	6
1936	GB	12	34	536	15.8	8
1937	GB	11	41	552	13.5	7
1938	GB	10	32	548	17.1	9
1939	GB	11	34	846	24.9	6
1940	GB	11	45	664	14.8	7
1941	GB	11	58	738	12.7	10
1942	GB	11	74	1211	16.4	17
1943	GB	10	47	776	16.5	11
1944	GB	10	58	866	14.9	9
1945	GB	10	47	834	17.7	9
TOTAL		**116**	**488**	**7991**	**16.4**	**99**

Hutson and the Packers lost to the Giants 23–17 in the 1938 NFL title game at the Polo Grounds (top), but Hutson's soft hands and blistering speed in the open field (opposite) carried him from Alabama (above) to Green Bay, where he helped usher in the modern passing game.

play," said the man who threw the pass, tailback Cecil Isbell.) In a game against the Detroit Lions in 1945, Hutson caught four touchdown passes and kicked five extra points for a total of 29 points in a single quarter, a record that still stands. Hutson scored a game-winning touchdown in his second outing as a Packer, and the play was unforgettable—an 83-yard touchdown pass from Arnie Herber on the first play from scrimmage against the Chicago Bears.

"He's a cagey and shifty gent," wrote John Kieran of *The New York Times*, "and when he runs out and throws up his arms, his fingers seem infused with some peculiar form of magnetism that unerringly draws flying leather in the form of a football." From 1935—when he joined the Packers after his two-touchdown performance in Alabama's 29–13 Rose Bowl victory over Stanford—until 1945, when he retired for the last time, Hutson dominated his position as no other player has. Indeed, he dominated his era as no other athlete, save Babe Ruth, has done. Hutson led the NFL in touchdown receptions nine times; he led in touchdowns and pass receptions eight times. In 1942, he caught a positively futuristic 74 passes. The Chicago Cardinal's Frank (Pop) Ivy finished second in receptions that year— with 27. It took 44 years for another receiver—Steve Largent of the Seattle Seahawks—to surpass Hutson's career record of 99 touchdown receptions, and Hutson got his 99 in an era when the forward pass was still being refined and NFL seasons were only 10 to 12 games long.

In those days, of course, no self-respecting football player spent half the game on the

sidelines. So Hutson, who was 6'1" tall and weighed 185 pounds, also played defensive end when he joined the Packers, and he was routinely trampled by the phalanx of blockers that protected runners coming out of the single wing. Lambeau, desperate to protect his precious asset, drafted South Carolina blocking back Larry Craig in 1939 and put him at defensive end, freeing up Hutson to play safety. The Antelope picked off 23 passes in his final four seasons, while simultaneously setting what may be an NFL record for retirements—five farewells between 1941 and his final goodbye in '45.

"I was trying to quit before I got killed," Hutson said later, but as stunningly elusive as he was on the field, that didn't seem likely. Hutson left after 11 pro seasons with three championships, two MVP awards, 193 points scored as a placekicker and a career total of 488 catches. He then got rich selling luxury cars in Racine, Wisc.

The man with the soft hands proved equally adept at the soft sell.   —J.G.

Hutson, who entered the pro football hall of fame in 1963, opened a successful automobile dealership (opposite, below) in Racine, Wisc., after he retired from the NFL, never to outrun a defensive back (above, left) or plow through an opponent's secondary (above, right) again.

Don Hutson was one of the legends we of a certain era grew up with. Greatest team: Chicago Bears. Greatest runner: Bronko Nagurski. Greatest receiver: Don Hutson. You didn't question it....

In 1989 I flew to Green Bay and spent an afternoon in the Packers' film room watching footage of Hutson.... What I saw was a Ray Berry on the possession routes, blessed with the grace of a Lynn Swann, plus a great hunger for the ball at the point of the catch, like a Jerry Rice. For 11 years—99 touchdowns, three championships, a pair of MVP awards—he was the best.

I ran one catch back frame by frame, an impossible reception on a sideline route. His momentum was pulling him out of bounds, but he somehow corkscrewed his body back in and kept extending his arms … and the ball stuck to his fingertips. I've seen only one other like it, Swann's against the Dallas Cowboys in the 1976 Super Bowl.

He was an unexplained force in the NFL, a meteor that lit up the sky. An original. A legend.

—PAUL ZIMMERMAN
July 7, 1997

"Hutson was almost
three times as productive
as any of his peers. No other
player in football history
can make that claim."

—*PETER KING, Sports Illustrated*

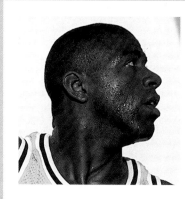

Magic Johnson

Earvin Johnson made us all believe in Magic. Not Harry Houdini magic, necessarily. More like Walt Disney magic. Johnson's calling card wasn't so much about prestidigitation as about the fairy tale atmosphere he created at the Great Western Forum. Heck, his beaming smile alone was enough to warrant the flashy nickname. Johnson's electric grin was so big it ate up half his face and reassured the world that, yes, basketball really was just a kid's game after all. Johnson's longtime Los Angeles Lakers teammate Kareem Abdul-Jabbar once defined charisma by simply pointing across the Lakers dressing room at No. 32. The cerebral center understood that Johnson was the perfect fit for the megawatt metropolis of L.A., captivating first the city and then the rest of the NBA during the glitzy decade of the 1980s.

From the moment the curtain rose on the Magic show, Johnson seemed born for the spotlight, which is odd for a guy who spent the first 20 years of his life in blue-collar Lansing, Mich., where his ethereal passing skills in the schoolyard earned him his famous title. Johnson led Everett High to a state championship as a senior, then signed with Michigan State, the hometown college. He led the Spartans to the NCAA championship two years later, when they defeated Indiana State and Larry Bird in the title game. Johnson left Michigan State for the pros after that sophomore season. As a climax to his incredible NBA rookie season he scored 42 points, grabbed 15 rebounds and made seven assists in the decisive Game 6 of the NBA Finals against the 76ers while filling in at center for the injured Abdul-Jabbar. That unexpected 1980 title finished off Johnson's unique trifecta. He had won titles at three levels in four years.

Magic's greatest trick was being a 6'9" point guard, a big man capable of playing the traditional little man's position. Hoop fans had never seen anything like this giant rumbling down the Forum floor leading a Lakers fast break, dishing behind his back or over his shoulder or sometimes threading a bounce pass nearly the length of the court. The phenomenon was dubbed Showtime, and Johnson was the director. Magic played all five positions at one time or another during his career, and could be an efficient scorer and rebounder. His range of talents was so

Johnson (opposite), who revolutionized the point guard position during his 12-year career, played the game with irrepressible joy.

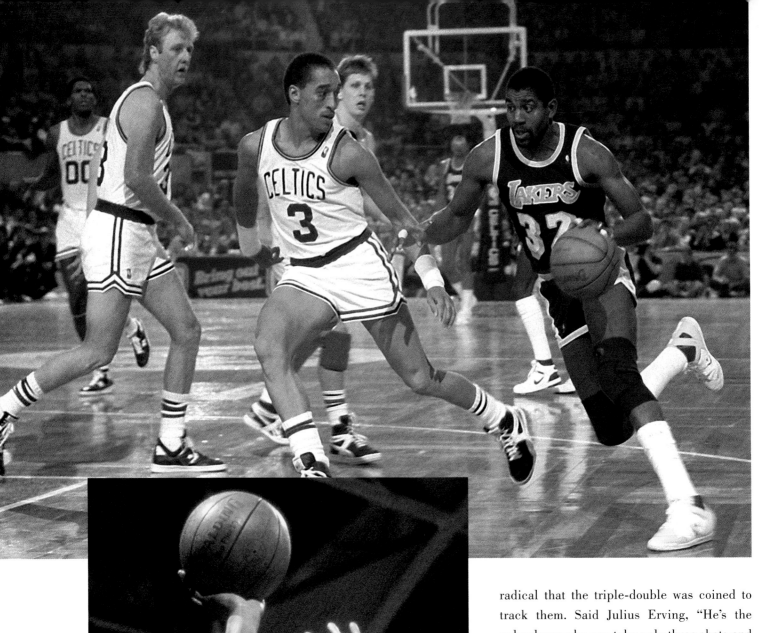

radical that the triple-double was coined to track them. Said Julius Erving, "He's the only player who can take only three shots and still dominate a game."

Johnson entered the NBA alongside Bird, and their careers would intertwine throughout the 1980s. Their intense rivalry almost single-handedly revived the floundering NBA. Bird's Boston Celtics and Johnson's Lakers would meet three times in the NBA Finals, with the Lakers winning twice. Between 1980 and '88, the Lakers won five titles and established themselves as the NBA's team of the decade. Johnson won three Finals MVP awards during the span.

Johnson's announcement on Nov. 7, 1991, that he had tested positive for HIV would

Johnson (top, with ball) had a fierce rivalry with the Celtics' Bird (top, second from left) that began when he led Michigan State (inset) to the 1979 NCAA title over Bird's Indiana State team, a winning habit Johnson (opposite) would maintain in the NBA.

"He's the best in the league. I'd pay to watch him play."
—LARRY BIRD

in SI's words

What defined the Lakers' Showtime fast-break style at its zenith was the way Magic sold his moves from the middle of the floor. Magic surely has the most expressive face in the history of sports. As he steamed toward the basket, his eyes would widen and his mouth would round into an O as he looked off his defender, selling the pass to, say, [Byron] Scott, on the right side and then suddenly zipping it over his shoulder to [James] Worthy on the left. The fast break is about making decisions in the wink of an eye, and Magic, like vintage [Bob] Cousy, made excellent ones while earning thousands of style points in the process.

Ultimately, the unique thing about Johnson as a player is that he was able to be at the cutting edge while still being somewhat old-fashioned. Until he slowed down a bit in recent seasons, he was the consummate playground player—the high dribble, the spin moves, the outside shot that looked like an afterthought. But even in his most electrifying moments he was, in contrast to [Michael] Jordan, never a particularly acrobatic player or a great leaper, especially as his knees grew more tender. Like [Larry] Bird, that other noted relic, he never had a classic jump shot, relying instead on an anachronistic one-hand set. And as the years rolled on, his signature shot became the hook, that hoary creation that he, like players of old, took—and made—with either hand. In deference to [Kareem] Abdul-Jabbar, he called it "the junior, junior skyhook." Magic was never just like Jordan, never just like Bird. He was somewhere in between, and thus attracted fans from both camps.

—JACK McCALLUM
Nov. 18, 1991

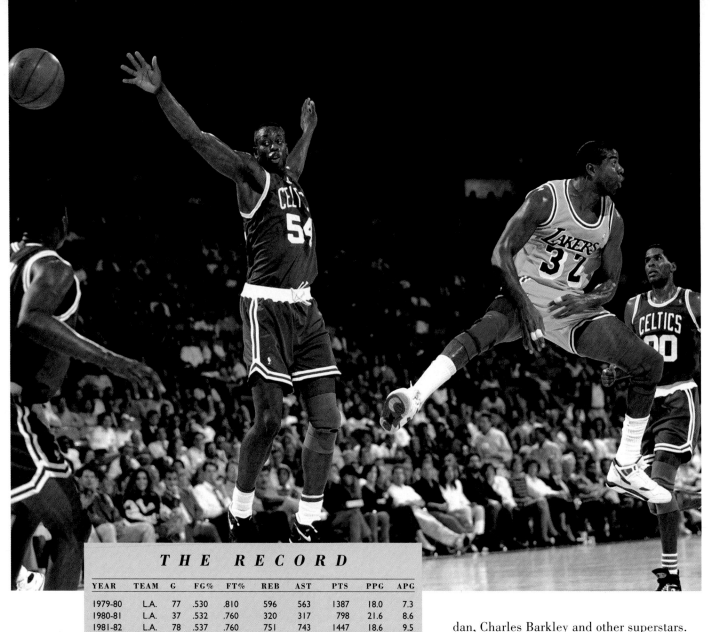

THE RECORD

YEAR	TEAM	G	FG%	FT%	REB	AST	PTS	PPG	APG
1979-80	L.A.	77	.530	.810	596	563	1387	18.0	7.3
1980-81	L.A.	37	.532	.760	320	317	798	21.6	8.6
1981-82	L.A.	78	.537	.760	751	743	1447	18.6	9.5
1982-83	L.A.	79	.548	.800	683	829	1326	16.8	10.5
1983-84	L.A.	67	.565	.810	491	875	1178	17.6	13.1
1984-85	L.A.	77	.561	.843	476	968	1406	18.3	12.6
1985-86	L.A.	72	.526	.871	426	907	1354	18.8	12.6
1986-87	L.A.	80	.522	.848	504	977	1909	23.9	12.2
1987-88	L.A.	72	.492	.853	449	858	1408	19.6	11.9
1988-89	L.A.	77	.509	.911	607	988	1730	22.5	12.8
1989-90	L.A.	79	.480	.890	522	907	1765	22.3	11.5
1990-91	L.A.	79	.477	.906	551	989	1531	19.4	12.5
1995-96	L.A.	32	.466	.856	183	220	468	14.6	6.9
TOTAL		**906**	**.520**	**.848**	**6559**	**10,141**	**17,707**	**19.5**	**11.2**

eventually lead to his premature retirement, but not before he made two memorable curtain calls: He was the MVP of the 1992 NBA All-Star Game, and he won an Olympic gold medal in Barcelona as a member of the original Dream Team featuring Bird, Michael Jor-

dan, Charles Barkley and other superstars.

Johnson's legacy is the redefinition of his position. He raised the requirements for elite point guard play, and he remains the standard by which the position is measured. While he will be remembered for his creative passing, he did sink one particularly memorable shot. Johnson won Game 4 of the 1987 Finals at the Boston Garden with an unlikely baby hook in the lane with two seconds left. He had copied the shot from Abdul-Jabbar, and he produced it from thin air at that crucial moment as if he was pulling a rabbit out of a hat. Like so many moments in Johnson's career, it was nothing short of Magic. —*T.C.*

No one ever threw the no-look pass with more style than Johnson (above), who, as a 20-year-old rookie one year removed from his NCAA triumph at Michigan State, led the Lakers to a six-game victory over the Philadelphia 76ers in the 1980 NBA Finals (opposite).

"He throws the ball behind his back, waves to the girls, has fun. But he's also a thug, barging into the boards, knocking people over. Maybe that's why he is Magic. Because now you see him, now you don't."
— PAUL WESTHEAD, *former coach of the Los Angeles Lakers*

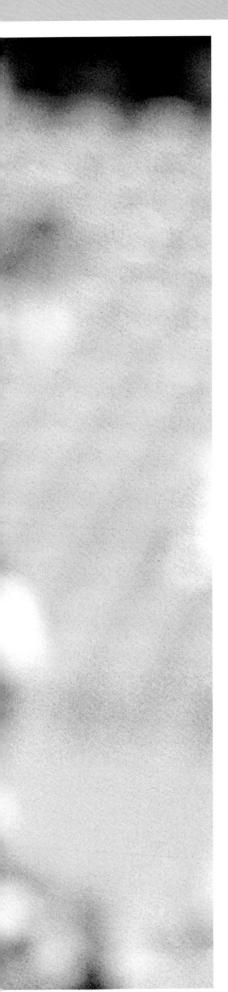

Jackie Joyner-Kersee

Other athletes competed in the heptathlon before Jackie Joyner-Kersee came along, but it was Joyner-Kersee who transformed the event into the Magnificent Seven. High and long jumps, 100-meter hurdles, 200-meter dash, 800-meter run, shot put and javelin— the heptathlon events demand an immense amount of skill, strength and speed from those who compete in them, and a staggering degree of same from those who excel in them. During her magnificent 18-year career, Joyner-Kersee conquered the seven like no one before or since.

The heptathlon seemed to have been invented solely for Joyner-Kersee, and judging by her electric smile on the track, no woman ever enjoyed competing in it more than JJK. But her prowess in track and field was not limited to the heptathlon. She repeatedly refused to give up her first love, the individual long jump, and for one year she and Heike Drechsler of Germany shared the world record in that event, which she once described as "like jumping for joy." Her

Named after Jacqueline Kennedy Onassis, Joyner-Kersee (left) became the First Lady of track and field, a world record–setting, versatile and durable performer who won medals in four Olympics.

"From the first day I saw Jackie, I knew she was the greatest woman athlete I'd ever seen. She had the eye for technique, the intent and the tenacity to be a world champion."
—*BOB KERSEE*

record of 24' 5½" was eventually eclipsed, but Joyner-Kersee never lost her love of the event.

When Jacqueline Joyner was born on March 3, 1962, in a declining neighborhood of East St. Louis, Ill., her grandmother urged her parents to name her after Jackie Kennedy in hopes that the baby would one day "be the First Lady of something." Jackie and her big brother Al, who would become a world-class triple jumper, vowed to escape from their blighted neighborhood. She spent countless hours honing her jumping ability by leaping

THE RECORD

OLYMPICS

YEAR	SITE	EVENT	FINISH	DIST./PTS
1984	Los Angeles	Heptathlon	Second	6385 pts.
1988	Seoul	Heptathlon	First	7291 pts. (WR)
1988	Seoul	Long Jump	First	24 ft. 3 ¼ in.(OR)
1992	Barcelona	Heptathlon	First	7044 pts.
1992	Barcelona	Long Jump	Third	23 ft. 2 ½ in.

WORLD CHAMPIONSHIPS

YEAR	SITE	EVENT	FINISH	DIST./PTS
1987	Rome	Heptathlon	First	7128 pts.
1987	Rome	Long Jump	First	24 ft. 1 ¼ in.
1991	Tokyo	Long Jump	First	24 ft. ¼ in.
1993	Stuttgart	Heptathlon	First	6837 pts.

OR=Olympic record; WR=world record

Joyner qualified at the U.S. Olympic Trials in 1984 (above) and finished second in the heptathlon at the Games in Los Angeles that year, a prelude to her performance in Barcelona in '92 (opposite), when she won the gold medal in the heptathlon and the bronze in the long jump.

off the front porch of the family house on Pig-gott Avenue into a sandpit fashioned by her sisters Angela and Debra, who toted the sand back from the local park in potato chip bags. Jackie began competing in local track meets at age nine and by the time she was 12 she had long jumped 17'3", tops in the nation for her age group. At age 14 she was the U.S. junior national champion in the pentathlon.

In her junior year at East St. Louis's Lincoln High School, Joyner set a state record in the long jump, and she also blossomed in basketball, leading Lincoln to the state championship. UCLA recruited Joyner for basketball, offering her a hoops scholarship. While she was named All-Conference in basketball, Joyner also made time for track and field. She focused on the long jump at first, but after failing to make the 1980 U.S. Olympic team in the event, she relented to Bruins assistant track coach Bob Kersee's insistence that she try the heptathlon.

Coach Kersee believed she had the poten-tial to be the world's greatest female athlete, and Joyner wasted no time fulfilling that promise: She won NCAA heptathlon titles in 1982 and '83, setting collegiate records both times. At the 1984 Olympic Games in Los Angeles, inspired by her brother Al's gold-medal performance in the triple jump, Jackie made a gallant run at the heptathlon gold but fell five points short.

She would win each of the next nine hep-tathlons she entered. In 1986, at the Good-will Games in Moscow, she became the first woman ever to top 7,000 points in the event. Less than a month later, at the U.S. Olympic Festival, she smashed her own record. The 1988 Olympics in Seoul became her personal stage. She won two golds, in the heptathlon (with a world-record 7,291 points) and in the long jump (24'3½"), to become the first multi-event winner in 64 years to also take an individual Olympic gold.

Joyner-Kersee won a third gold in the hep-tathlon in Barcelona in 1992, prompting

"She's the best athlete ever, man or woman. She's also the most normal person ever. I mean, she shops at Pik 'n' Save. But it's more than that. People like Jackie because she's human."
—*SHELIA BURRELL, heptathlete*

1976 Olympic decathlon champion Bruce Jenner to call her the best athlete on the planet. Finally, in her Olympic farewell in Atlanta in '96, Joyner-Kersee suffered a leg injury that forced her to withdraw from the heptathlon. She was in sixth place before her final attempt in the long jump but somehow summoned the strength and courage to leap past three competitors and into third. It was a wonderfully fitting end to her Olympic career: Ailing, all but counted out, the irrepressible Joyner-Kersee made one final jump for joy—and a bronze medal.

Joyner-Kersee won 12 consecutive heptathlons over a six-year span from 1986 to '91, and in her career the First Lady of track and field won 25 of the 36 heptathlons she entered, including her final competition at the 1998 Goodwill Games. After winning that gold medal, Joyner-Kersee wept on the shoulder of her longtime coach, who during her career had also become her husband and her most passionate fan. "Jackie's performances are like a great opera," Bob Kersee once said. "I feel like I should be wearing a tux when I watch them." —*T.C.*

Joyner-Kersee won the heptathlon at the 1987 world championships in Rome (above) before reaching her career peak at the 1988 Olympics in Seoul, where she won the long jump (opposite) and the heptathlon, with a world-record total of 7,291 points.

in SI's words

She interrupted the night's clatter with a quiet, graceful farewell, a gently resonating harp's chord played in the midst of a rock concert.... [Jackie] Joyner-Kersee stood at the end of the long jump runway, sixth in a field of eight, with only the last of her six attempts remaining. Her right leg was wrapped from knee to mid-thigh, a bandage supporting the same fickle hamstring that six days earlier had forced her tearful withdrawal from the heptathlon, an event in which she had won the gold medal in the previous two Olympics.... And as she began her run, she looked every day of her 34 years.

She had won five Olympic medals before this, the same number as Evelyn Ashford and Florence Griffith Joyner, but since her heptathlon gold and long jump bronze in Barcelona four years ago, her body has slowly broken down. After her withdrawal from the heptathlon, President Clinton phoned with his condolences; the call took on the feel of a long-deserved goodbye.

... "I said to myself, 'This is it, Jackie, this is it,'" said Joyner-Kersee. "'This isn't the way you wanted it to be, but this is your last shot. If the leg is going to pull, it's going to pull.' I just wanted to give it my best effort." She tore down the runway and left the takeoff board on her wounded leg, reached back with her hands as she fell toward the sand and desperately extended her legs. Her distance was 22' 11¾", a bronze medal by one inch.

—TIM LAYDEN
Aug. 3, 1996

Joe Louis

Joe Louis was often outnumbered when he entered the boxing ring. He always had to contend with his opponent, and on several occasions the great Louis also went toe-to-toe with Adolf Hitler or Emperor Hirohito, Benito Mussolini or the Ku Klux Klan. And he knocked them all senseless, bringing new meaning to the phrase "champion of the world." Though this burden was more a product of the turbulent times in which he ascended to fame than the result of Louis's activism, the champ was nevertheless compelled to pulverize people for a good cause. He mixed left jabs with constitutional rights, and for two decades he strove to be better than every other man just to prove that all men are created equal.

Louis was not a rabble-rouser. He was a shy kid whose mother sent him off to violin lessons after school; however, he stashed his boxing gloves in the violin case and secretly tutored in the sweet science instead. By age 20 Louis was the national AAU light-heavyweight champ, groomed to be an emotionless knockout machine who meticulously stalked his victim before taking the poor guy out with either hand. Louis began his pro career with 27 straight victories, including 23 knockouts, and became the youngest heavyweight champion ever. He then engineered the longest reign in that title's history. For 12 dominant years from 1937 to 1949, Louis won 25 title defenses, with more of them ending in the first round (five) than going the distance (three). Most challengers simply surrendered, as did ex-champ Max Baer, who was counted out in the fourth round even though he was fully conscious and propped on one knee. Baer admitted afterward, "I could have struggled up once more, but when I get executed people are going to have to pay more than $25 a seat to watch it."

Louis almost always went for the knockout because his trainer, Jack Blackburn, repeatedly warned him that, as only the second black heavyweight champ ever, he'd be wise not to leave his fate to the judges in this white man's sport. While many blacks looked upon Louis as a symbol of power for the powerless, the white media initially treated him as a cartoon curiosity, referring to him in print as everything from "the mahogany maimer" to the "the coffee-colored KO king"

Louis stopped the lightly regarded Lou Nova (opposite) in the sixth round of their heavyweight title fight in New York City on Sept. 29, 1941.

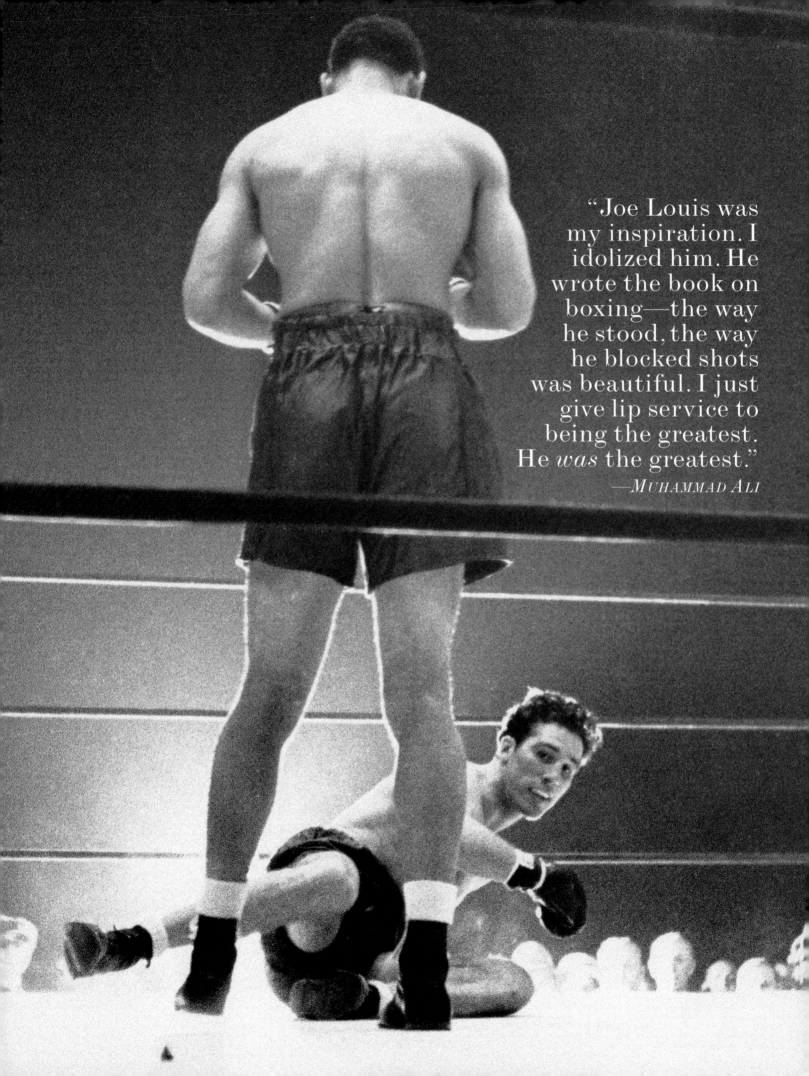

"Joe Louis was my inspiration. I idolized him. He wrote the book on boxing—the way he stood, the way he blocked shots was beautiful. I just give lip service to being the greatest. He *was* the greatest."
—*MUHAMMAD ALI*

before settling on the equally derogatory "Brown Bomber."

Louis made his first political statement with a 1935 knockout of the bruising Primo Carnera of Italy—a body blow to Mussolini, who at the time was threatening to invade Ethiopia, one of the few independent black nations on the globe. After Louis had suffered his first defeat at the hands of Germany's Max Schmeling in 1936, the rematch two years later was hyped as a preview to the impending World War. President Franklin Roosevelt invited Louis to the White House for a pep talk, and Americans were transfixed as never before by the outcome of a sporting event. In front of 70,000 fans at Yankee Stadium, Louis needed just 124 seconds to

Louis scored 49 knockouts in his career, including a first-round decking of Buddy Baer (top) in 1942, a second round KO of Johnny Paychek (above) in 1940 and, perhaps most memorable of all, a 13th-round pasting of Billy Conn (opposite) in their famous 1941 title bout in New York City.

Update

The conventional assumption about Joe Louis's life after boxing is that he was an unsophisticated naif, manipulated and exploited by the fight game, who ended up, if not alone and penniless, then ruined and humiliated by financial problems.

The truth is far more complex, and considerably less bleak.

Louis died on April 12, 1981, the day after he attended the Larry Holmes–Trevor Berbick heavyweight title fight at Caesars Palace, where the 4,000 fight fans in atten-

dance gave him a standing ovation. Though he had indeed squandered the money he earned as a fighter, was troubled by well-publicized tax debts and had a history as a philanderer, Louis was happy in his twilight years. He had overcome psy-

chological problems he suffered in the early 1970s, and he lived in Las Vegas with his third wife, Martha Jefferson, a successful attorney. Louis worked at Caesars Palace as an official greeter, for which he was paid an annual salary of $50,000 and provided with a house with a swimming pool.

Many observers apparently deemed this position degrading to the great fighter, but Louis was comfortable in the role. As for his financial indiscretions—the champ had spent the bulk of his money on others, supporting several brothers and sisters and a hefty entourage of pals, donating to black causes, lavishing gifts on friends—Louis reportedly told a friend, cheerfully, that even if he had boxed in the more lucrative fight game of the 1960s, it "wouldn't make no difference. I'd still end up broke." Clearly, to Louis, money was for spending, not saving. In his 1978 autobiography, *My Life*, Louis wrote, "Nobody took advantage of me … I danced, I paid the piper, and left him a big fat tip."

THE RECORD

WORLD HEAVYWEIGHT CHAMPIONSHIP FIGHTS

DATE	WINNER	LOSER	RESULT	SITE
June 22, 1937	Joe Louis	James J. Braddock	KO 8	Chicago
Aug 30, 1937	Joe Louis	Tommy Farr	UD 15	New York City
Feb 23, 1938	Joe Louis	Nathan Mann	KO 3	New York City
Apr 1, 1938	Joe Louis	Harry Thomas	KO 5	Chicago
June 22, 1938	Joe Louis	Max Schmeling	KO 1	New York City
Jan 25, 1939	Joe Louis	John Henry Lewis	KO 1	New York City
Apr 17, 1939	Joe Louis	Jack Roper	KO 1	Los Angeles
June 28, 1939	Joe Louis	Tony Galento	TKO 4	New York City
Sept 20, 1939	Joe Louis	Bob Pastor	KO 11	Detroit
Feb 9, 1940	Joe Louis	Arturo Godoy	TKO 8	New York City
Mar 29, 1940	Joe Louis	Johnny Paychek	KO 2	New York City
June 20, 1940	Joe Louis	Arturo Godoy	TKO 8	New York City
Dec 16, 1940	Joe Louis	Al McCoy	TKO 6	Boston
Jan 31, 1941	Joe Louis	Red Burman	KO 5	New York City
Feb 17, 1941	Joe Louis	Gus Dorazio	KO 2	Philadelphia
Mar 21, 1941	Joe Louis	Abe Simon	TKO 13	Detroit
Apr 8, 1941	Joe Louis	Tony Musto	TKO 9	St. Louis
May 23, 1941	Joe Louis	Buddy Baer	DQ 7	Washington, DC
June 18, 1941	Joe Louis	Billy Conn	KO 13	New York City
Sept 29, 1941	Joe Louis	Lou Nova	TKO 6	New York City
Jan 9, 1942	Joe Louis	Buddy Baer	KO 1	New York City
Mar 27, 1942	Joe Louis	Abe Simon	KO 6	New York City
June 9, 1946	Joe Louis	Billy Conn	KO 8	New York City
Sept 18, 1946	Joe Louis	Tami Mauriello	KO 1	New York City
Dec 5, 1947	Joe Louis	Jersey Joe Walcott	Split 15	New York City
June 25, 1948	Joe Louis	Jersey Joe Walcott	KO 11	New York City
Sept 27, 1950	E. Charles	Joe Louis	UD 15	New York City

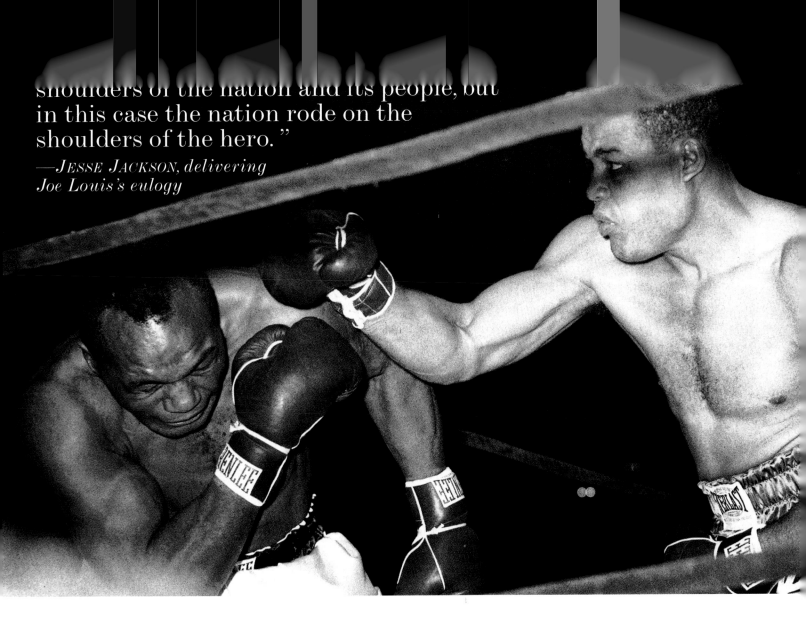

shoulders of the nation and its people, but in this case the nation rode on the shoulders of the hero."

—*JESSE JACKSON, delivering Joe Louis's eulogy*

Louis visited soldiers in a British hospital during World War II (opposite, above) then returned to the U.S. to defend his title four more times, including on Dec. 5, 1947, when he won a split decision over Jersey Joe Walcott (above), before retiring in 1948 to focus on his golf game (opposite, below).

demolish the man touted as "the Heil Hitler hero." The victory was so lopsided that the Nazi government pulled the plug on the broadcast before the German public could hear about the vicious right to the kidney that ended the fight, fractured one of Schmeling's vertebra and sent him to the hospital.

After that bout, Louis assumed his role as the first black American hero embraced by all races. He would again become an emblem of national unity in 1942, when he volunteered for the Army, fought bouts to benefit the war effort and talked tough about socking it to the Japanese for the bombing of Pearl Harbor.

When Louis finally retired from the ring in 1951 with a record of 63–3 and 49 knockouts, he represented the end of an era of segregation in American sports. His presence helped blacks gain entry into pro baseball, basketball and football. In fact, a full decade before Jackie Robinson began playing for the Brooklyn Dodgers, Louis's knockouts broadcast by radio gave African-Americans hope that they too could enjoy the American Dream. Louis's profound influence is evident in the words of renowned white sportswriter Jimmy Cannon, who wrote of Louis, "He's a credit to his race … the human race." —*T.C.*

Mickey Mantle

Any observant student of '50s culture will immediately notice the iconic power of the initials "M.M." In Hollywood, a small-town girl named Norma Jean became a film fantasy called Marilyn Monroe during the decade, while in New York a raw Oklahoma kid named Mickey Mantle became a baseball legend. They had more in common than initials, too. Both were ill-prepared for the stratospheric heights to which their fame catapulted them, and both would lose themselves in substance abuse.

Indeed, many observers wondered how much better Mantle, a switch-hitting power hitter with good speed, might have been if he hadn't been so enamored of the bottle. His stylistic signature was a go-for-the-suburbs swing that often left him twisted like a rubber toy—his belt buckle facing the dugout, his back facing the pitcher and his face facing the umpire. To Little Leaguers who fought for the right to wear his uniform No. 7, Mantle's swing was a manifesto, a balletic demand for no salad but extra dessert, two days of school with five-day weekends and free Tootsie Rolls on request. Mantle struck out a lot—he whiffed 126 times in 1959—but his fans didn't care. They lived for his tape-measure home runs. Not that any conventional tape stretched to 565 feet, the estimated distance of the tater Mantle knocked out of Washington's Griffith Stadium in 1953.

Power, of course, was a '50s theme. Postwar America was growing into its role as the greatest economic and military power in the world, and the two M.M. icons represented the power of personality and sexuality, of beauty, skill and brawn. Mantle was the most powerful hitter in the most popular American sport, and he played for the most powerful team, the New York Yankees, who won 12 American League pennants and seven World Series during his 18 years with the team. In Mantle's Triple Crown season, 1956, he belted 52 homers, drove in 130 runs and batted .353 to serve undeniable notice to Yankees fans that a suitable successor to the great Joe DiMaggio had been located.

Marketers, a relatively new and increasingly rabid breed in the 1950s, did not fail to notice the budding superstar in centerfield at Yankee Stadium. Of the three merchandise

A 16-time All Star, Mantle (opposite) barely missed a beat after his 1956 Triple Crown season, batting .363 with 34 homers and 94 RBIs in 1957.

THE RECORD							
YEAR	TEAM	G	R	HR	RBI	SB	AVG
1951	NY-A	96	61	13	65	8	.267
1952	NY-A	142	94	23	87	4	.311
1953	NY-A	127	105	21	92	8	.295
1954	NY-A	146	129	27	102	5	.300
1955	NY-A	147	121	37	99	8	.306
1956	NY-A	150	132	52	130	10	.353
1957	NY-A	144	121	34	94	16	.365
1958	NY-A	150	127	42	97	18	.304
1959	NY-A	144	104	31	75	21	.285
1960	NY-A	153	119	40	94	14	.275
1961	NY-A	153	132	54	128	12	.317
1962	NY-A	123	96	30	89	9	.321
1963	NY-A	65	40	15	35	2	.314
1964	NY-A	143	92	35	111	6	.303
1965	NY-A	122	44	19	46	4	.255
1966	NY-A	108	40	23	56	1	.288
1967	NY-A	144	63	22	55	1	.245
1968	NY-A	144	57	18	54	6	.237
TOTAL		2401	1677	536	1509	153	.298

monsters in baseball—Mantle, Willie Mays and Duke Snider, the centerfielders for the three dominant teams—Mantle's name was the most profitable. His signature appeared on baseball gloves, bats and baseball cards whose value would climb astronomically through the years.

Sadly, Mantle was overmatched by such fame. He was the son of an Oklahoma lead miner who died of Hodgkin's disease in 1951, when Mickey's big-league career was just getting underway. Although Mantle had a reputation as a clubhouse prankster, he was at heart a morose and fatalistic type. But he often brightened up with the aid of a few beers or cocktails. With his Yankees teammates Billy Martin and Whitey Ford, Mantle became a

Mantle had the speed to bunt for a base hit (opposite) when necessary, but when he came to bat during his 1956 Triple Crown season (above), in which he batted .353 with 52 homers and 130 RBIs, most pitchers expected, and feared, that he would swing away.

"He can run, steal bases, throw, hit for average, and hit with power like I've never seen. Just don't put him at shortstop."
—HARRY CRAFT, *minor league manager, on Mantle*

habitué of Manhattan's Copacabana nightclub, and took stubborn pride in his ability to punish his body both on and off the field. ("If I had known I would live this long," he said famously when he was in his 50s, "I would have taken better care of myself.") Like Monroe, Mantle seemed lost at times.

The miracle was how little Mantle let his misgivings and his alcoholism interfere with his game. Chronically injured—he suffered his first serious knee injury in the '51 World Series—Mantle played in pain for most of his career. And he excelled, turning out MVP seasons in '56, '57 and '62. His teammate, Jim Bouton, recalled in his book *Ball Four*

how an injured and hungover Mantle once uncorked a pinch-hit home run in a day game and plodded around the bases while the fans stood and cheered. Returning to the dugout, Mantle sat down heavily and said, "Those people don't know how tough that really was."

When the Mick was halfway healthy, he played with reckless, and effective, abandon. He ran on catchers and outfielders with a kind of joyful contempt, and he covered Yankee Stadium's huge center field with ease. And whenever one of his 536 career homers cleared the fence, Mantle's face lit up with a grin, happy to be part of a game that could lift his spirits and make the world go away.

—*J.G.*

Mantle (opposite, below) always swung with gusto, as he demonstrated in 1961 against Detroit while belting his 49th homer of the year (above), and in '64 in the Bronx, when he hit his record 16th career World Series home run (opposite, above) to win Game 3 against the Cardinals.

in SI's words

Mickey Mantle, with his death Sunday at 63, passes from these pages forever and becomes the property of anthropologists, people who can more properly put the calipers to celebrity, who can more accurately track the force of personality. We can't do it anymore, couldn't really do it to begin with. He batted this, hit that. You can look it up. Hell, we do all the time. But there's nothing in our library, in all those numbers, that explains how Mantle moves so smoothly from baseball history into national legend, a country's touchstone, the lopsided grin on our society.

He wasn't the greatest player who ever lived, not even of his time perhaps.... But for generations of men, he's the guy, has been the guy, will be the guy. And what does that mean exactly? A woman beseeches Mantle, who survived beyond his baseball career as a kind of corporate greeter, to make an appearance, to surprise her husband. Mantle materializes at some cocktail party, introductions are made, and the husband weeps in the presence of such fantasy made flesh. It means that, exactly.

—RICHARD HOFFER
Aug. 21, 1995

"No man in the history of baseball had as much power as Mickey Mantle. No man. When you're talking about Mickey Mantle— it's an altogether different level. Separates the men from the boys."
—*BILLY MARTIN*

Willie Mays

Willie Mays wore a baseball cap that didn't fit and sat perched atop his head like a crown. It was not so much a fashion statement as a dramatic device. The hat was choreographed to fly off just as Mays rounded second base on one of his breathtaking sprints from first to third or midway through his graceful pursuit of a line drive to the gap. New York Giants fans ate it up.

Mays was always an unabashed showman. When he switched to the basket catch early in his big league career it wasn't because that method was simpler, but because it appeared more daring. In the batter's box, on the base paths or in centerfield, Mays created the illusion of jeopardy when in fact he was a baseball magician, supremely confident that the woman he was sawing in half would emerge intact. Mays was such a crowd pleaser that when he was first called up to the majors in 1951 after 35 games with the AAA Minneapolis Millers, his departure proved so devastating to Millers fans that the Giants felt compelled to place an advertisement of apology in the Minneapolis newspapers.

Mays readily acknowledged that much of his flair was inherited. He was the grandson of an Alabama sharecropper who moonlighted in the black amateur baseball leagues and the son of Willie Mays Sr., who was known as Kitty Kat for his agile skill in local semipro games. Willie Jr. began his professional career at age 14 and two seasons later played for the Birmingham Black Barons of the Negro major leagues. When Jackie Robinson broke baseball's color line with the Brooklyn Dodgers in 1947, he cracked the door open for Mays to sign with the Giants in 1950.

In a parable of perseverance still spoon-fed to young prospects half a century later, Mays produced only one hit in his first 26 major league at-bats. He wept and asked Giants manager Leo Durocher to send him back to Minneapolis, but Durocher refused, and Mays regrouped to win the rookie of the year award in 1951. After missing most of the next two seasons while serving in the army, Mays returned in 1954 to lead the majors in batting average and slugging percentage, punctuating that season in Game 1 of the World Series against Cleveland with

Despite losing almost two seasons to military service, the great Mays (opposite) belted 660 home runs in his career, third on the alltime list.

the Catch. His full speed over-the-shoulder grab of Vic Wertz's rocket some 440 feet into deepest centerfield at the Polo Grounds is considered the spark that ignited the Giants' Series sweep. Moments after the catch, commonly called the most spectacular defensive play in baseball history, Mays informed teammate Monte Irvin, "I had that one all the way."

Modeling his game after Joe DiMaggio, whom Mays idolized as the sport's most versatile star, Mays's career statistics rank with the best: 660 home runs, a .302 batting average and 11 Gold Gloves. Mays also became the first player ever to crack 300 homers and steal 300 bases. Had Mays not those two years to the military and spent 14 seasons in San Francisco's windswept Candlestick Park—the Giants' home after they left New York—many baseball experts, including Mays himself, suspect that he would have broken Babe Ruth's home run record before Hank Aaron did. When Bob Dylan released his second album, in 1963,

Mays finished up his career with the New York Mets (opposite, below), but it was as a member of the Giants that he made his mark, scoring runs (above), stealing bases (opposite, top), hitting and fielding so well that many experts call him the greatest all-around baseball player ever.

THE RECORD

YEAR	TEAM	G	R	HR	RBI	SB	AVG
1951	NY-N	121	59	20	68	7	.274
1952	NY-N	34	17	4	23	4	.236
1954	NY-N	151	119	41	110	8	.345
1955	NY-N	152	123	51	127	24	.319
1956	NY-N	152	101	36	84	40	.296
1957	NY-N	152	112	35	97	38	.333
1958	SF-N	152	121	29	96	31	.347
1959	SF-N	151	125	34	104	27	.313
1960	SF-N	153	107	29	103	25	.319
1961	SF-N	154	129	40	123	18	.308
1962	SF-N	162	130	49	141	18	.304
1963	SF-N	157	115	38	103	8	.314
1964	SF-N	157	121	47	111	19	.296
1965	SF-N	157	118	52	112	9	.317
1966	SF-N	152	99	37	103	5	.288
1967	SF-N	141	83	22	70	6	.263
1968	SF-N	148	84	23	79	12	.289
1969	SF-N	117	64	13	58	6	.283
1970	SF-N	139	94	28	83	5	.291
1971	SF-N	136	82	18	61	23	.271
1972	SF-N	19	8	0	3	3	.184
	NY-N	69	27	8	19	1	.267
	YR	88	35	8	22	4	.250
1973	NY-N	66	24	6	25	1	.211
TOTAL		**2992**	**2062**	**660**	**1903**	**338**	**.302**

"Willie Mays could do everything and do it better than anyone else [and] with a joyous grace."
—ARTHUR DALEY, *sportswriter*

he spoke for all National League pitchers when he sang, "What do you do about Willie Mays?" in the song "I Shall Be Free."

About the only errors Mays ever committed occurred when he tried to remember people's names, which prompted him to greet almost everybody with a generic "Say hey." He was therefore dubbed the Say Hey Kid because he played baseball with the name, the high-pitched voice and the innocent joy of a little leaguer. In fact, after many home games at the Polo Grounds, Mays would walk the few blocks back to Sugar Hill in Harlem and join a stickball game with the children in his neighborhood. Mays whacked prodigious five-sewer moonshots with his landlady's broomhandle, swinging with such delighted might that he sometimes came out from under his cap.

He had us all the way. —T.C.

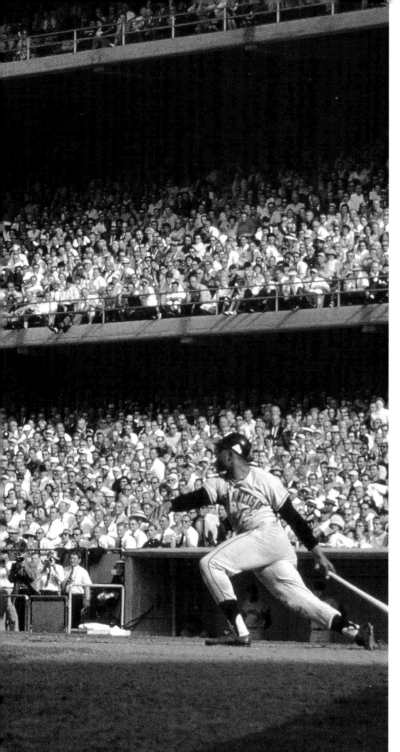

Spotlight

Willie Mays's famous catch of a drive to dead center by Cleveland's Vic Wertz in Game 1 of the 1954 World Series is his—and possibly baseball's—most famous catch, but the Say Hey Kid has another grab to his credit that some say was better than the celebrated catch against the Indians. It happened in 1951, Mays's rookie season, during a Giants–Pirates game at Pittsburgh's Forbes Field. Deepest left-center field at Forbes was 457 feet from home plate, and when a Pirates batter launched a tracer in that direction, Mays gave chase. As he reached the warning track, he realized the ball was hooking to his right. If he had stopped and tried to reach across his body with his glove hand, he would have missed the ball and given up a double, at least. Mays's solution? He flipped up his bare right hand and—smack—made the catch. After the game, Pirates general manager Branch Rickey, who had been in baseball for 48 years, sent Mays a note telling him, "That was the finest catch I have ever seen and the finest catch I ever hope to see."

"There's an aesthetic quality to how a crowd *enjoys* Willie Mays. When he walks in front of a ballpark of 40,000 people, the stands come down. No other player but DiMaggio evokes that kind of feeling of, well, *Willie Mays*."
—AL ROSEN, *Giants executive and former Cleveland Indians third baseman*

Mays saw baseball as "a form of show business," and he always had time for his fans (above, right); in 1962 (opposite, left) he belted 49 homers and helped the Giants reach the World Series by hitting a key home run in a playoff against the Dodgers (above, center).

Joe Montana

Hollywood couldn't have written a script any better than Joe Montana's reality. Here was an underdog quarterback with a cowboy name and azure eyes who time and again yanked his team back from the brink of disaster. Think Indiana Jones in shoulder pads.

For sheer entertainment value, Montana was as hard to beat as the teams he quarterbacked. During his illustrious football career he staged an extraordinary number of fourth-quarter comeback victories everywhere from the Cotton Bowl to the Super Bowl. He made 31 of them in his NFL days. "When the game is on the line and you need someone to go in there and win it right now, I would rather have Joe Montana than anyone who ever played the game," said Bill Walsh, who coached Montana for 10 years in San Francisco. "He's got this resourcefulness, this something that's hard to put into words."

Montana's greatness was always a little hard to describe. Though he grew up in western Pennsylvania, a land known for producing Hall of Fame quarterbacks, he was unlike local brethren Joe Namath and Dan Marino because he didn't look as though he was minted at the football factory. A spindly 6'2", 190 pounds when he arrived at Notre Dame in 1974, he languished as low as seventh on the quarterback depth chart. But three years later, Montana would lead his team to a national championship, and in 1979, in his college grand finale, he orchestrated the sort of rally for which he would become renowned. Battling the University of Houston in an ice storm at the 1979 Cotton Bowl, Montana and Notre Dame trailed 34–12 with less than eight minutes remaining in the game. Suffering from hypothermia, Montana chugged some boullion and rallied the Irish to a wildly improbable 35–34 victory. He completed the final touchdown pass with two seconds to play, capping one of the most dramatic comebacks in college football history.

Montana then set his sights on the NFL, whose scouts traditionally judge quarterbacks more by size and arm strength than by courage or the amount of ice in their veins. His arm rated "average," Montana lasted until the third round, when the San Fran-

Bay Area treasures: Montana (opposite), who led the 49ers to four Super Bowls, ranks with the Golden Gate Bridge in the hearts of San Franciscans.

> "He's like Lazarus. You roll back the stone, Joe limps out—and throws for 300 yards."
> —TIM McKYER, former 49ers cornerback

THE RECORD

YEAR	TEAM	G	ATT	COMP	COMP%	YDS	TD	INT	RATING
1979	SF	16	23	13	56.5	96	1	0	81.1
1980	SF	15	273	176	64.5	1795	15	9	87.8
1981	SF	16	488	311	63.7	3565	19	12	88.4
1982	SF	9	346	213	61.6	2613	17	11	88.0
1983	SF	16	515	332	64.5	3910	26	12	94.6
1984	SF	16	432	279	64.6	3630	28	10	102.9
1985	SF	15	494	303	61.3	3653	27	13	91.3
1986	SF	8	307	191	62.2	2236	8	9	80.7
1987	SF	13	398	266	66.8	3054	31	13	102.1
1988	SF	14	397	238	59.9	2981	18	10	87.9
1989	SF	13	386	271	70.2	3521	26	8	112.4
1990	SF	15	520	321	61.7	3944	26	16	89.0
1991	DNP								
1992	SF	1	21	15	71.4	126	2	0	118.4
1993	KC	11	298	181	60.7	2144	13	7	87.4
1994	KC	14	493	299	60.6	3283	16	9	83.6
TOTAL		192	5391	3409	63.2	40551	273	139	92.3

cisco 49ers selected him with the 82nd overall pick. Three seasons later, Montana steered the previously woeful 49ers to a 13–3 record. In the 1981 NFC championship game, he submitted the first chapter of his NFL masterpiece. He had a little help on this one, though. Trailing Dallas 27–21, Montana drove the Niners 89 yards to the Dallas 6-yard line. On third down, with 58 seconds on the clock, he couldn't find an open receiver so he lofted a pass that he later admitted was intended to fly out of the end zone. Somehow, 49ers receiver Dwight Clark leapt high enough to snag the ball, and San Francisco punched its ticket to Super Bowl XVI. Ironically, the most legendary single play of Montana's career would be written into NFL lore not as the Throw, or the Drive, but as the Catch.

Two weeks later, Montana completed 14 of 22 passes, and the 49ers beat Cincinnati 26–21 for their first NFL championship.

Montana and the Niners got by the Lions in the 1983 playoffs (opposite), but lost a thriller to Washington in the NFC title game that year, a disappointment they would redeem the following year by going 15–1 and routing the Miami Dolphins 38–16 in Super Bowl XIX (above).

"What really impressed us was that he could immediately put into practice any coaching suggestion. He would literally eat the words right out of your mouth. Call it what you will—intelligence, intangibles, charisma—that's what we saw in Joe."
—SAM WYCHE, *former Niners quarterbacks coach*

in SI's words

He somehow seems to breathe slower when everyone else breathes fast, seems to have a different metabolism. Remember that final drive in the 1989 Super Bowl? You fell off the chair. ... He completed one pass, and then another, and another. Eight of nine passes during the drive. Was there ever any better high-pressure bit of football business? Didn't you read what he said at the start of the drive?

"Hey check it out," he said to tackle Harris Barton.

"Check what out?" Barton asked.

"There, in the stands, standing near the exit ramp," Joe said.

"There's John Candy."

Wasn't that the greatest? There are lists of the comebacks he has quarterbacked in 12 seasons with the Niners and four college seasons at Notre Dame. The lists are so long that they look like the itinerary for a breakout tour by a heavy-metal band. Your father remembers reading about someone named Chip Hilton who did the same things Joe does. Your grandfather mentions someone named Frank Merriwell. You don't know any of that. Weren't those characters from fiction? Joe is real. A real Joe.

—LEIGH MONTVILLE
Dec. 24, 1990

Undersized and underrated at the start of his career at Notre Dame (above, left), Montana, surrounded by such players as the great Rice (above, right), and receiver Clark (opposite, No. 87), would go on to spearhead the 49ers dynasty and the celebrated West Coast offense.

Montana ran for one touchdown and threw for two more and was named MVP of the game. Over a nine-year span from 1982 to '90, Montana led San Francisco to four Super Bowls, all of which they won. On the biggest stage of all, he completed 68% of his passes for 1,142 yards and 11 touchdowns without throwing a single interception. He was named the Super Bowl MVP a record three times. In Super Bowl XXIII Montana engineered the greatest drive in the history of the big game, a 92-yard march in which he carved up the Bengals defense with short, quick passes to receiver Jerry Rice and running back Roger Craig. He completed eight precision throws on the 11-play drive. The coup de grâce came when, with 39 seconds left, he zipped a 10-yard pass to John Taylor as the receiver slanted into the end zone to give the 49ers a breathtaking 20–16 triumph.

The enduring image of Montana comes from that evening in Miami, his wiry arms extended skyward in celebration of yet another fourth quarter miracle. He retired from the NFL at the end of the 1994 season with 273 touchdown passes over 15 seasons. The kid with the average arm would leave the NFL with the second highest passer rating in league history. Montana was just a regular Joe who turned into into Joe Cool thanks to his knack for creating the game's most precious commodities—Hollywood happy endings. —*T.C.*

Martina Navratilova

Nothing about Martina Navratilova was ordinary, from her physique to her talent, from her tennis style to her life style. While existing just beyond the baseline of what had come to be the norm in tennis, Navratilova earned respect both for her astounding athletic success and because she reached the summit without ever compromising herself. "I like the fact that she's honest," rival Gabriela Sabatini once said of her. "She is how she is and nothing else, both on and off the court. She's not hiding anything."

Growing up in a small town in Czechoslovakia, hidden behind the Iron Curtain, Navratilova neither comprehended nor fit the stereotypes of her time. She never tried to be the perky, girlish tennis prodigy that fans of the game had come to expect; instead she fanatically built her body and won with raw power. She defected to America at age 18 and endured six years as a woman without a country, until she became a United States citizen in 1981. Nine days later, she acknowledged publicly that she was bisexual.

Even the compelling personal details of her life, however, could never distract us from what she accomplished on the court. No other tennis player, male or female, has won as many tournaments as Navratilova. In 1982 and '83 she won 176 times in singles and lost only four times. The next year she ran off a magnificent stretch of 74 straight victories that is considered the most dominant run in tennis history. During the 14-month period from the 1983 Wimbledon through the 1984 U.S. Open, she won six consecutive Grand Slam titles, tying the record set by Margaret Smith Court. Navratilova achieved all of this while bridging the eras of two of her sport's most celebrated champions in the primes of their careers. After losing 21 of the first 25 matches in her extraordinary rivalry with Chris Evert, Navratilova concluded their head-to-head series with a 43–37 edge. And later, in the closing stages of her career, Navratilova won nine of 18 matches against Steffi Graf, including the '87 Wimbledon final.

If any place truly felt like home during Navratilova's tennis odyssey, it was probably the staid and traditional manicured lawn of Centre Court at Wimbledon, where she won half of her 18 Grand Slam singles titles.

Navratilova (opposite) served up 74 straight victories in 1984 and won 167 singles titles in her career, more than any other player, male or female.

"Martina revolutionized the game by her superb athleticism and aggressiveness, not to mention her outspokenness and her candor."
—CHRIS EVERT

Although Navratilova and Wimbledon could hardly have been an odder couple, they came to complement each other like strawberries and cream. Early in her career, Navratilova said she hoped to surpass Bjorn Borg's modern record of five consecutive Wimbledon titles, and she did, winning six straight silver plates from 1982 to '87. Her very grand total of nine Wimbledon singles titles is more than any player's ever. After winning her first in 1978 she said, "I feel so many emotions, I don't know what to do first: laugh or cry or scream."

She did a little of each, and brought a welcome dose of passion to the sometimes robotic world of professional tennis. Her approach on the court was as paradoxical as her life off of it. Despite learning the game on slow red clay, she took control of the sport with her daring, left-handed serve-and-volley game that ended many of her service points in three strokes, refreshing efficiency in a world of baseline

Navratilova, who won her fourth Wimbledon in 1983 (opposite), returned to her native Czechoslovakia with the U.S. Federation Cup team in 1986 (above, left), one year before defeating her legendary rival Evert (above, right) en route to a historic sixth straight Wimbledon title.

> ## "She'll be remembered as the best ever. She has pushed the next generation to be better, and that's each generation's responsibility."
> *—Billie Jean King*

THE RECORD

YEAR	AUS	FRENCH	WIM	U.S.
	S-D-M	S-D-M	S-D-M	S-D-M
1974	0-0-0	0-0-1	0-0-0	0-0-0
1975	0-0-0	0-1-0	0-0-0	0-0-0
1976	0-0-0	0-0-0	0-1-0	0-0-0
1977	0-0-0	0-0-0	0-0-0	0-1-0
1978	0-0-0	0-0-0	1-0-0	0-1-0
1979	0-0-0	0-0-0	1-1-0	0-0-0
1980	0-1-0	0-0-0	0-0-0	0-1-0
1981	1-0-0	0-0-0	0-1-0	0-0-0
1982	0-1-0	1-1-0	1-1-0	0-0-0
1983	1-1-0	0-0-0	1-1-0	1-1-0
1984	0-1-0	1-1-0	1-1-0	1-1-0
1985	1-1-0	0-1-1	1-0-1	0-0-1
1986	0-0-0	0-1-0	1-1-0	1-1-0
1987	0-1-0	0-1-0	1-0-0	1-1-1
1988	0-1-0	0-1-0	0-0-0	0-0-0
1989	0-1-0	0-0-0	0-0-0	0-1-0
1990	0-0-0	0-0-0	1-0-0	0-1-0
TOTAL	**3-8-0**	**2-7-2**	**9-7-1**	**4-9-2**

teenyboppers and endless rallies. Also, despite being larger than most of her competition, she was the tour's best athlete, covering the entire court better than anyone.

After 11 years in exile, Navratilova finally returned to Czechoslovakia in 1986 as a member of the U.S. Federation Cup team, and though barely acknowledged by the government, she was hailed as a heroine by the Czech people. American crowds had adopted her as well, and when her 22-year career officially ended with a loss to Sabatini in the first round of the 1994 Virginia Slims Championships in New York's Madison Square Garden, a banner bearing the name of the greatest women's tennis player of all time was hoisted to the rafters. After all those years, the 38-year-old Navratilova echoed the sentiments she felt as a bewildered 21-year-old Wimbledon champ by saying, "I don't know whether to laugh or cry." The emotions were the only part of tennis she never mastered.

—*T.C.*

Navratilova reached the final of her last Wimbledon in 1994 (above) and took a tuft of grass as a memento from Centre Court, where she won nine singles titles, including the 1979 championship (opposite), a 6–4, 6–4 defeat of Evert Lloyd.

in SI's words

Navratilova wasn't seriously challenged until [the injured] Gigi Fernandez gimped onto the court for their semifinal match [which Navratilova won, 6–4, 7–6, to reach the final].... It seemed only right that the greatest champion Wimbledon has ever known have a final run on the lawn. "This is what I wanted: to go out in style," said Navratilova.

With Princess Diana, singer k.d. lang and South African deputy president F.W. de Klerk all attending the women's final, she did. But her bond with Wimbledon goes deeper than royalty. "This court," Chris Evert once said, "is her court."

... [After Conchita Martínez won the final 6–4, 3–6, 6–3 someone] yelled, "Come back next year, Martina!" but she shook her head no and blew a kiss.

... She trod on tradition by circling the court—the first time anyone could remember a loser taking the champion's stroll—and the Centre Court crowd stood and saluted Navratilova with the day's best sound. At 4:20 p.m. she moved toward the door, curtsied, then broke off to collect a last few blades of grass. Seventy-five minutes later she walked out of the club entrance, climbed into a car and rolled slowly away. Two girls closed the black iron gates behind her.

—S.L. PRICE
July 11, 1994

Photo Credits

FRONT COVER
Hardcover, clockwise from top left: AP (Mantle); Corbis-Bettmann (Brown); Neil Leifer (Ali); John Biever (Jordan); Horrace Tonge/London Sunday Times (Laver); Paul J. Bereswill (Gretzky); Corbis-Bettmann (Didrikson); John Biever (Montana).

Softcover, clockwise from left: Peter Read Miller XX40601; Bill Smith X41515; AP; Paul J. Bereswill.

BACK COVER
From left to right: Ronald C. Modra; George Tiedemann; Sheedy & Long; Corbis-Bettmann.

FRONT MATTER
1, Hy Peskin/FPG; 2-3, David E. Klutho.

INTRODUCTION
6, George Tiedemann; 7, Sheedy & Long.

TRANSCENDENT THREE
8-9, Brian Drake; 10, Corbis-Bettmann; 11, Walter Iooss Jr.; 12, Tony Triolo; 13, Neil Leifer; 14, Flip Schulke; 15, Neil Leifer; 16, Neil Leifer; 17, Corbis-Bettmann; 18, George Silk; 19, Neil Leifer; 20, Richard Mackson; 21, John Biever; 22 left, Rich Clarkson; right, Bill Smith; 23, Manny Millan; 24, Walter Iooss Jr.; 25 right, Manny Millan; left, John Biever; 26, Andy Hayt/NBA Photos; 27 top, Walter Iooss Jr.; bottom, John W. McDonough; 28, Corbis-Bettmann; 29, Baseball Hall of Fame Library; 30, AP/Baseball Hall of Fame Library; 31 top, Corbis-Bettmann; bottom, Baseball Hall of Fame; 32, Corbis-Bettmann; 33 left, Corbis-Bettmann; right, Baseball Hall of Fame.

PEERLESS PERFORMERS
34-35, Neil Leifer; 36, UPI/Corbis-Bettmann; 37, Corbis-Bettmann; 38, Walter Iooss, Jr.; 39, Neil Leifer; 40 bottom, Corbis-Bettmann; 41, AP; 42, Walter Iooss Jr.; 43, Sheedy & Long; 44, Corbis-Bettmann; 46 both, Corbis-Bettmann; 47, Corbis-Bettmann; 48, Corbis-Bettmann; 49, Corbis-Bettmann; 50, Paul J. Bereswill; 51, Andy Hayt; 52, David E. Klutho; 53, Andrew D. Bernstein; 54, Paul J. Bereswill; 55, David E. Klutho; 56, Horrace Tonge/London Sunday Times; 57, James Drake; 58, Corbis-Bettmann; 59, AP; 60, Gary Cranham; 61, Gary Cranham; 62, Walter Iooss Jr.; 63, Heinz Kluetmeier; 64, Neil Leifer; 65, Heinz Kluetmeier; 66, Bill Frakes; 67, Steve Powell; 68, James Drake; 69, Dick Garrett/Columbus Citizen; 70, Leviton-Atlanta; 71, Rich Clarkson; 72, Richard Mackson; 73 right, Jacqueline Duvoisin; left, John Iacono; 74, Neil Leifer; 75, Paulo Muniz/Life; 76 right, Jerry Cooke; left, George Tiedemann; 77, Jerry Cooke; 78, Photo Trends; 79, Neil Leifer; 80, Sheedy & Long; 81, John G. Zimmerman; 82, Walter Iooss Jr.; 83, Sheedy & Long; 84, Walter Iooss Jr.; 85 top, Fred Kaplan; bottom, Dick Raphael; 86, Corbis-Bettmann; 88, Culver Pictures; 89, Culver Pictures; 90, Corbis-Bettmann; 91, Cumberland County Historical Society; 93, Leonard McCombe/Life; 94 left, Leonard McCombe/Life; right, Hy Peskin; 95, Richard Meek; 96, Hy Peskin; 97 both, Hy Peskin.

GREATNESS VISIBLE
98-99, Mike Powell/Allsport; 100, Naismith Memorial Basketball Hall of Fame; 101, Corbis-Bettmann; 102, Neil Leifer; 103, Fred Kaplan; 104, Neil Leifer; 105, Neil Leifer; 106 top, Tony Triolo; bottom, James Drake; 107, John G. Zimmerman; 108, Manny Millan; 110, John Iacono; 111, John W. McDonough; 112, Rich Clarkson; 113, Andrew D. Bernstein; 114, Walter Iooss Jr.; 115, Neil Leifer; 116, Neil Leifer; 117, Neil Leifer; 118 both, Neil Leifer; 119, Neil Leifer; 120, The New York Times; 121, The New York Times; 122, Brown Brothers; 123 both, Corbis-Bettmann; 124, Corbis-Bettmann; 125, Culver Pictures; 126, UPI/Corbis-Bettmann; 127, NFL Photos; 128 top, UPI/Corbis-Bettmann; bottom, Bryant Museum, University of Alabama; 129, NFL Photos; 130, NFL Photos; 131 top, UPI/Corbis-Bettmann; bottom, NFL Photos; 132, Walter Iooss Jr.; 133, Walter Iooss Jr.; 134 top, Dick Raphael; bottom, Heinz Kluetmeier; 135, Peter Read Miller; 136, John W. McDonough; 137, Rich Clarkson; 138, Tony Duffy/Allsport; 140, Manny Millan; 141, John Biever; 142, Tony Duffy/Allsport; 143, Tony Duffy/Allsport; 144, Corbis-Bettmann; 145, New York Daily News; 146, AP; 147 both, AP; 148 top, US Army Photo; bottom, AP; 150, AP; 151, Art Rickerby; 152, Art Daley; 153, Richard Meek; 154, AP; 155 top, AP; bottom, Mark Kauffman; 156, Hy Peskin; 157, Walter Iooss Jr.; 158, Richard Meek; 159 top, Richard Meek; bottom, Neil Leifer; 160 both, Neil Leifer; 161, Neil Leifer; 162, Peter Read Miller; 163, Albert Watson; 164, Mickey Pfleger/Endzone; 165, Andy Hayt; 166, Richard Mackson; 167 left, Tony Tomsic; right, John Biever; 169, Ronald C. Modra; 170, Walter Iooss Jr.; 171 left, Ronald C. Modra; right, Russ Adams; 172, Bill Frakes; 173, Tony Duffy.

Index

A
Aaron, Hank **1**, 7, **102**, **103**, **104**, **105**, **106**, **107**
Abdul-Jabbar, Kareem 6, 7, 100, 132, 135, 136
Air Jordan 20, 25
Alabama, University of 126, 129
Ali, Muhammad 6, 7, 10, **12**, **13**, **14**, **15**, **16**, **17**, **18**, **19**, 42, 79 146
Allen, George 126
Amer-I-Can 114, 117
Arthur Ashe Stadium 58
Ashford, Evelyn 143
Atlanta Braves 104, 105, 106, 107
Atlanta Hawks 26
Auerbach, Red 81, 83, **85**, 112

B
Baer, Buddy **147**
Baer, Max 144
Ball Four 154
Baltimore Colts 117
Bannister, Roger 6
Barkley, Charles 136
Barton, Harris 166
Baugh, Sammy 100
Baurú, Brazil 76
Baylor, Elgin **83**
Beamon, Bob 7, 65
Beckenbauer, Franz 77
Bellamy, Walt 40
Berg, Patty 49
Berbick, Trevor 148
Berkow, Ira 39
Berry, Raymond 131
Bettmann, Gary 7
Big Dipper 39, 41, 42
Bingham, Walter 71
Bird, Larry **6**, 7, 75, 100, **108**, **109**, **110**, **111**, **112**, **113**, **132**, **134**, 135, 136
Birmingham Black Barons 157
Black Economic Union 114
Blackburn, Jack 144
Blount, Roy Jr. 57, 58
Borg, Bjorn 171
Boston Celtics 20, 23, 39, 41, 42, 81, 82, 83, 109, 111, 112, 113, 134
Boston Garden 20, 23, 113, 136
Boston Red Sox 30, 92, 94, 95, 97
Boswell, Tom 69
Bouton, Jim 154
Bridges, Bill 81
Brooklyn Dodgers 149, 157
Brown, Jim 75, **114**, **115**, **116**, **117**, **118**, **119**
Brown, Paul **117**
Bryant, Bear 126
Budge, Don 57, 58
Burdette, Lew 105
Burrell, Shelia 142
Button, Dick 6

C

Caesars Palace 148
Candlestick Park 158
Candy, John 166
Cannon, Jimmy 32, 149
Canton Bulldogs 91
Carew, Rod 92
Carnera, Primo 147
Chamberlain, Wilt 7, 36, **38, 39, 40, 41, 42, 43, 80, 82**
Champaign, Illinois 122
Chasing the Dream Foundation 107
Chicago Bears 125, 129, 131
Chicago Bulls 20, 22, 25, 26, 27, 113
Chicago Cardinals 122, 129
Chicago Cubs 32, 95
Chuvalo, George **12**
Cincinnati Bengals 165, 167
Clark, Dwight 165, **166**
Clay, Cassius Marcellus Sr. 13
Cleveland Browns 114
Cleveland Cavaliers 22
Cleveland Indians 31, 94, 157, 161
Cleveland Rams 126
Clinton, Bill 143
Cobb, Ty 6, 30, 100
Comaneci, Nadia 6
Conn, Billy **146**
Copacabana 154
Cotton Bowl 163
Court, Margaret Smith 100, 168
Cousy, Bob 85, 110, 111, 135
Craft, Harry 153
Craig, Larry 130
Craig, Roger 167
Creamer, Robert 29, 33
Cronin, Joe 92
Cunningham, Billy 41

D

Daley, Arthur 159
Dallas Cowboys 116, 131, 165
Dawkins, Darryl 6
De Brito, Valdemar 75
de Klerk, F.W. 173
Debringer, John 29
Deford, Frank 82
DeLoach, Joe 65
Dempsey, Jack 100, 120
Detroit Lions 164
Didrikson, Babe 36, **44**, 45, **46, 47, 48, 49**
DiMaggio, Joe 92, 95, **101**, 150, 158
Disney, Walt 132
Downing, Al **106**
Dream Team 136
Drechsler, Heike 139
Drummond, John 67
Durocher, Leo 157
Dylan, Bob 158

E

Edison, Thomas 75
Edmonton Oilers 51, 52, 54
Els, Ernie 72
Embry, Wayne 40
Emerson, Roy **59**
Erving, Julius 134
Everett High School 132
Evert, Chris 100, 168, **171**, 173
Ewry, Ray 66

F

Fenway Park 92, 94
Fernandez, Gigi 173
Fogolin, Lee 54
Folley, Zora **16**
Forbes Field 161
Ford, Whitey 152
Foreman, George 14, 15, 17
Frazier, Joe 13, 17, **19**
French Lick, Indiana 109, 110
Frick, Ford 122
Fulton County Stadium 107

G

Gallico, Paul 45
Galloping Ghost 122
Gehrig, Lou 32, **33**, 100
Georgetown University 20
Giants Stadium 79
Gibson, Bob 103
Glavine, Tom 107
Glenn, John 92
Golden Gate Bridge 163
Goodwill Games
 1986, 141
 1998, 142
Gorgeous George 13
Gowdy, Curt 96
Graf, Steffi 100, 168
Graham, Otto 100
Grange, Red 100, **120, 121,** 122, **123, 124, 125**
Green Bay Packers 126, 128, 129, 130, 131
Great Western Forum 132
Gretzky, Wayne **2, 3**, 7, 10, 36 **50, 51, 52, 53, 54, 55**, 100
Griffith Joyner, Florence 143
Griffith Stadium 150
Grout, Jack 69

H

Halas, George 122, 124, 125
Hauser, Thomas 19
Havlicek, John 42, 82
Hayes, Elvin 81
Heinsohn, Tommy 82
Henie, Sonja 6
Herber, Arnie 129
Hilton, Chip 166
Hirohito, Emperor 144
Hitler, Adolf 144
Hoad, Lew 57, 58
Hoffer, Richard 155
Hogan, Ben 6, 49
Holmes, Larry 148
Holyfield, Evander 19

Home Run: My Life in Pictures 107
Hopman, Harry 57
Houdini, Harry 132
House of David (baseball team) 49
Houston, University of 163
Howe, Gordie 6, 50, 54, 100
Howell, Dixie 126
Hudlin, Willis 31
Huff, Sam 118
Hutson, Don 100, **126, 127, 128, 129, 130, 131**

I

Illinois, University of 120
Indiana Pacers 113
Indianapolis Clowns 106
Indiana State University 110, 112, 132
Indiana University 27, 110
Irvin, Monte 158
Isbell, Cecil 129
Ivy, Frank "Pop" 129

J

Jackson, Jesse 149
Jackson, Mark 113
Jaeger, Andrea 172
Jefferson, Martha 148
Jenner, Bruce 142
Jim Thorpe—All-American 88
Johnson, Ben 64
Johnson, Magic 100, 111, 113, **132, 133, 134, 135, 136, 137**
Johnson, Rafer 6
Jolson, Al 120
Jones, Bobby 6, 69
Jones, C.M. 59
Jones, Janet 54
Jones, Sam 82
Jordan, Lee Roy 116
Jordan, Michael 6, 7, **11, 20, 21, 22, 23, 24, 25, 26, 27,** 36, 113, 135, 136
Joyner, Al 140, 141
Joyner, Angela 141
Joyner, Debra 141
Joyner-Kersee, Jackie 6, 46, 100, **138**, 139, **140, 141, 142, 143**
Justice, David 107
Juventus (football club) 78

K

Kansas, University of 40
Kansas City Chiefs 42
Kennedy Onassis, Jacqueline 139, 140
Kersee, Bob 140, 141, 142
Kieran, John 129
King, Billie Jean 6, 100, 172
King Gustav V 86, 91
King, Peter 131
Kiviat, Abel 89
Knight, Bob 27
Koenig, Mark 32
Kram, Mark 19

Kuhn, Bowie 107
Ku Klux Klan 144

L

Ladies Professional Golf Association (LPGA) 48, 49
Lambeau, Curly 126, 130
lang, k.d. 173
Lanier, Bob 43
Largent, Steve 129
Laver, Rod **7**, 10, 11, **56, 57, 58, 59, 60, 61**, 100
Layden, Tim 143
Lewis, Carl 36, 62, **63, 64, 65, 66, 67**
Lewis, Carol 62
Lidz, Franz 33
Lilly, Bob 116
Lincoln High School 141
Liston, Sonny 13, 14, **18**
Lopez, Nancy 6
Los Angeles Kings 52, 53, 54
Los Angeles Lakers 39, 42, 111, 132, 134, 135, 136
Los Angeles Raiders 118
Louis, Joe 7, 100, **144, 145, 146, 147, 148, 149**

M

Madison Square Garden 22, 172
Magnani, Dante 126
Magnavox Corporation 103
Malone, Karl 6, 25
Mantle, Mickey 100, **150, 151, 152, 153, 154, 155**
Man o' War 120
Mara, Tim 122
Maravich, Pete **110**
Marino, Dan 6, 163
Maris, Roger 33
Mars Attacks! 117
Martin, Billy 152, 155
Martinez, Conchita 173
Masters, Edgar Lee 112
Mauch Chunk, Pennsylvania 90
Mays, Willie 103, 152, **156, 157, 158, 159, 160, 161**
McCallum, Jack 90, 111, 135
McGuire, Frank 40
McEnroe, John 100
McGwire, Mark 6
McIlvanney, Hugh 15
McKyer, Tim 165
Menke, Frank G. 45
Merriwell, Frank 166
Miami Dolphins 165
Michigan, University of 122
Michigan State University 111, 132, 134
Miller, Reggie 113
Milwaukee Braves 103
Minneapolis Millers 157
Mitchell, Dennis 65
Modell, Art 114, 117
Monroe, Marilyn 150, 154
Montana, Joe 10, 100, **162, 163, 164, 165, 166, 167**

Montville, Leigh 166
Morehouse College 107
Moses, Edwin
Mussolini, Benito 144, 147

N

Nagurski, Bronko 131
Namath, Joe 163
National Association for the
Advancement of Colored People
(NAACP) 107
Navratilova, Martina 100, **168,
169, 170, 171, 172, 173**
NBA Finals
 1967, 39
 1972, 39
 1973, 42
 1980, 132, 137
 1987, 136
 1992, 22
 1993, **23**
 1997, 22, 26
 1998, 25, 26
NCAA Basketball Championship
 1955, 85
 1956, 85
 1979, 110, 132
 1982, 20
Neale, Greasy 128
Negro Leagues 103, 104, 106
Nelson, Byron 6
Nelson, Lindsey 123
Nevers, Ernie 100
Newcombe, John 57, 61
New York Cosmos 76, 79
New York Giants (baseball) 157,
158, 160, 161
New York Giants (football) 114,
117, 118, 122, 125
New York Islanders 52, 54
New York Knicks 22, 25, 39, 42,
113
New York Mets 159
New York Rangers 54
New York Yankees 32, 94, 150,
152, 154, 155
Nicklaus, Jack 36, **68, 69, 70,
71, 72, 73,** 100
Ninowski, Jim **118**
North American Soccer League
76, 79
North Carolina, University of 20,
22,
Northwestern University 42
Norton, Ken **17**
Notre Dame, University of 163,
166, 167
Nova, Lou **145**
Nurmi, Paavo 100, 120

O

Oerter, Al 6, 66, 67
Olympics
 1912, 86, 90
 1932, 46, 49
 1936, 64
 1948, 88
 1956, 82
 1960, 13, 14
 1972, 6
 1984, 64, 140, 141
 1988, 64, 141, 142
 1992, 65, 66, 136, 140, 141, 143
 1996, 65
O'Meara, Mark 71, 72
100 Rifles 114
O'Neil, Buck 103
One Minute to Play 123
Original Gangstas 117
Overbrook High School 40
Owens, Jesse 64, 100

P

Palmer, Arnold 69, **71,** 100
Passeau, Claude 95
Paychek, Johnny **147**
Pelé 6, 7, 11, **74, 75, 76, 77,
78, 79**
Philadelphia 76ers 39, 42, 137
Philadelphia Athletics 92
Philadelphia Eagles 128
Philadelphia Flyers 52
Philadelphia Warriors 39, 40
Pippen, Scottie 27, 113
Pittsburgh Pirates 161
Polo Grounds 125, 128, 158, 160
Portland Trailblazers 22
Povich, Shirley 33
Powell, Mike 65
Price, S.L. 173
Price, Vincent 88
Princess Diana 173

Q

Quadros, Janio 78

R

Reilly, Rick 67, 69, 71
Rice, Grantland 88, 91, 125
Rice, Jerry 6, 100, 131, **167**
Rickey, Branch 161
Riggs, Bobby 100
Robertson, Oscar 6, 7, **100**
Robinson, Jackie 100, 103, 149,
157
Robinson, Sugar Ray 100
Roche, Tony 57, 58, 59
Rodgers, Phil 72
Roosevelt, Franklin Delano 147
Root, Charlie 32
Rose, Jalen 113
Rose Bowl 126, 129
Rosen, Al 161
Rosewall, Ken 57, 58, 61
Roth, Werner 78
Rudolph, Mendy **84**
Rudolph, Wilma 100
Ruklick, Joe 42
"Rumble in the Jungle" 14
Runyon, Damon 120
Russell, Bill 36, 39, 40, **80, 81,
82, 83, 84, 85**
Russell, Bryon 25

Ruth, Babe 6, 7, **10,** 26, **28, 29,
30, 31, 32, 33,** 45, 75, 103,
104, 106, 107, 120, 129

S

Sabatini, Gabriela 168, 172
St. Louis Cardinals 45, 155
Sampras, Pete 100
San Francisco, University of 85
San Francisco 49ers 163, 165,
166, 167
San Francisco Warriors 41
Santos (football club) 76, 78, 79
Sarazen, Gene 49, 72
Sather, Glen 52
"Say Hey Kid" 160
Schapp, Dick 107
Schmeling, Max 147
Scioto Country Club 69
Scott, Byron 135
Seattle Seahawks 129
Seattle Sounders 79
Seattle SuperSonics 25
Shirley, Jean 49
Smits, Rik 113
Snead, J.C. 70
Snider, Duke 152
South Carolina, University of 130
Spitz, Mark 6
Stanford University 129
Stanley Cup Finals
 1984, 52
 1985, 52
 1993, 54
Super Bowl
 X 131
 XVI 165
 XIX 165
 XXIII 167
Stockton, John 25
Swann, Lynn 131
Syracuse University 114

T

Taylor, John 167
Tellez, Tom 67
Texas Tornado 45
Thompson, Daley 6
Thorpe, Jim 36, **86, 87, 88,
89, 90, 91**
Thorpe, Patricia Askew 90
"Thrilla in Manila" 19
Thurmond, Nate 40
Trevino, Lee 71
Turner Field 107

U

UCLA 141
Uecker, Bob 42
Underwood, John 61, 122
United Center 20
Updike, John 92
Utah Jazz 22, 25

V

Vietnam War 14

W

Walcott, Jersey Joe **149**
Walker, Chet 41
Walsh, Bill 163
Warner, Glenn "Pop" 86
Washington Redskins 126, 165
Watson, Tom 71, 72
Welch, Raquel 114
Wertz, Vic 158, 161
Wilkins, Dominique 111, 120
Williams, Cleveland **15**
Williams, Ted **36,** 82, **92, 93,
94, 95, 96, 97**
Wolfley, Ron 119
Wooten, John **118, 119**
World Hockey Association 50, 54
World Cup
 1958, 75, 76, 78
 1962, 75
 1970, 79
World Series
 1932, 32
 1951, 154
 1954, 157, 161
 1964, 155
Worthy, James 135
Wrigley Field 32, 122
Wyche, Sam 166

Y

Yankee Stadium **116,** 147, 150,
154
Young, Andrew 106

Z

Zimmerman, Paul 131